wayward
spirits
&
earthbound
souls

About the Author

Anson V. Gogh has been helping lost souls cross into the light for over a decade. She and her daughter have the ability to tune in to what wayward spirits most desire and convince them that this longing can be satisfied "on the other side of the light." Sometimes the work is heartwarming, sometimes frustrating, but it is always satisfying. Gogh is also a practicing Wiccan, and has studied various religions and philosophies over the years.

After first discovering that she had this talent, Gogh did research and path-walking to improve her skills. In the course of her research, she noted that there were few sources that aimed to provide practical insight into how to cross ghosts. This book is the result.

We are all teachers, and we are all students.

Anson V. Gogh

wayward
spirits
&
earthbound
souls

true tales of ghostly crossings

Llewellyn Publications
Woodbury, Minnesota

First Edition
First Printing, 2010

Book design by Steffani Sawyer
Cover design by Kevin R. Brown
Cover images: tree © Photos.com/Jupiter Images; woman © Masterfile Corporation

Llewellyn is a registered trademark of Llewellyn Worldwide, Ltd.

Library of Congress Cataloging-in-Publication Data
Gogh, Anson V., 1961–
  Wayward spirits & earthbound souls: true tales of ghostly crossings /
Anson V. Gogh.
    p. cm.
  ISBN 978-0-7387-1935-1
  1. Ghost stories, American. I. Title.
  PS648.G48G64 2010
  133.1—dc22
                                    2009027474

Llewellyn Publications
A Division of Llewellyn Worldwide, Ltd.
2143 Wooddale Drive, Dept. 978-0-7387-1935-1
Woodbury, Minnesota 55125-2989, U.S.A.
www.llewellyn.com

Printed in the United States of America

This book is dedicated to my son, daughter, and fiancé. Thank you for your belief in me and your love and support.

To Nicky and Madison, who have already gone home, and to puppy Shiloh (who will follow them, but not too soon we hope), and especially to the rat, Socrates, thank you all for being part of this book. And to all the other pets I have and have ever had … you make our lives so much richer.

Contents

Contents

Foreword

"I see dead people" is a line most Americans are familiar with, but few actually ever get to say. Those who do see dead people are rarely able to comprehend their own truth, and they hide in psychiatric care or crack houses to escape the torment, never seeming to find a way to reconcile the two realities they live in.

Ironically, this conflict between physical and spiritual realities is the very dilemma that lost spirits suffer. I've learned that they are unable to leave the physical behind, to leave loose ends untied, or even to believe they are worthy of going into the light. So they stay—attached to the physical and the mundane, angry, lost, and confused. They become a member of a parallel existence known as *waywards*.

At the core of the tales in this book is a family that refuses to ignore what they see, what they feel, what they know. Who accept that nonphysical reality is also real. Lost souls share our limited space, and deserve the same compassion we feel for our physical counterparts who suffer the pains of living. Anson V. Gogh's family experiences the same desire to help waywards that most people feel when seeing a lost child. We just want to help them get home.

This is what Anson does—helps waywards go home.

Wayward spirits live fairly normal lives, as bodiless entities can, and cast their energy onto those who share physical space with them. They rearrange things, open and close things, and take things, while we blindly accept such occurrences as the result of our own absentmindedness, or simply dismiss them as things that could happen on their own. Is it really important how the washing machine moved a few inches away from the wall? Or what exactly the cat is chasing down the hall at 2:00 AM? Or how that envelope ended up on the floor?

We, as physical beings, see only what we already believe in. We find rational explanations for unexplained phenomena, and always find answers convenient to our belief system. We don't see ghosts. We think that those who claim to see ghosts are nut cases. And yet, on warm summer nights, we have no explanation for the chill that shivers through the moist air, raising the hair on the nape of our neck.

As if someone is watching…

My personal experience with waywards is not one full of bright lights or shaking furniture, or even of bumps in the night. It is simply about results.

My family had moved into a century-old house that we knew had a sordid past. For a few years, our house's environment just never seemed to become home. Although it was barely discernible, we could sense a hostility in the air, a vacuum that seemed to swallow the very essence of positivity from the house. But we managed to live a fairly normal life there.

Anson first visited our house when her fiancé was installing new flooring, and she began sending waywards home. She did this on her own, not sharing any of her activities with us. We simply assumed she was exploring our unique house. Only when she was finished did she tell with us about her work. Deep down, I scoffed and judged her a whack job. Harmless, but still a whack job.

Months later, my relatives came to visit. They had been here to see the flooring going in, but hadn't returned since the cleansing ("cleansing" is perhaps not a very respectful term, but I'm not really schooled in the proper terms). They immediately starting fawning over the "feel" of the house.

"Everything seems at peace here," my mother said to me. "All the work you've done since we were here last has really made this house feel like a home!"

As I tried to think of which work she might be referring to, I realized that no new work had actually been done, since we'd put other projects on hold until the floors were finished.

Her simple observation got me making a mental inventory. What factors were different, that might explain this new feeling that we were now aware of? We knew it was true as soon as my mother said it, so we must have felt it for a while. We just hadn't recognized it before.

This became the moment of my enlightenment. Anson's work was the only thing that was different in the house, and although we had never seen a wayward or believed in ghosts, we realized that we were the beneficiaries of her calling.

We may never comprehend what Anson sees, but we can no longer deny that she sees it. I believe that readers will also have to walk this fine line to see the truth behind these writings, and suspend any preconceived notions. My family accepts that Anson travels a different path than we do, but we believe that path to be righteous.

For those with the gift of sight, this book is a how-to.

For those without the gift, this book removes the blinders.

Journey knowingly into this realm.

—Mark Swickard
January 2009

We analyzed work, and love, and life.
Paint and curtains and furniture.
Everything was the same.

Acknowledgments

I would like to thank the Wiccan lady and the medicine woman for their knowledge and help with crossing my first wayward. Did you know what I was getting into? I also appreciate Darlene, and Lee and her husband Luis, for reading some of the stories in this book and giving me helpful criticism.

A huge thank you goes out to all the physical people who encountered the waywards whose stories are in this book. You all helped me to learn from the ghosts as well as from you. And, of course, to our astral friends who helped with a lot of our crossings, a huge thank you. You all know who you are.

Also a big thank you to all my coworkers, both past and present; I love you all. Without your love, support, humor, and enthusiasm I would have a lot less fun and laughter in my life.

A special thank you to Speed Bump for keeping me safe that first year we worked together. And to Mark: thank you for reading the whole book and for being so kind and putting up with "a harmless whack job."

Last, but certainly not least, a big thank you to my daughter and fiancé for your love, support, and encouragement. You both stood beside me, laughed with me, cried with me. I can't begin to tell you how much this kind of love means to me. Thank you from the bottom of my heart. I love you.

Introduction

So ... what is this book about? It is about helping souls who are locked in their own prison open the door and go home. This may be done quickly, or, as in a few of the stories I share, it can take some time. Most of the earthbound souls I've encountered take a few hours or even a few days before they are ready to cross to the other side. I hope that when you finish reading this book, you will have a better understanding of what a ghost truly is and be able to help these unfortunate souls go home.

First, let me clarify what I mean by the term *wayward*. A wayward is the soul of a person who is stuck in the physical plane of existence, or "goes wayward," after the death of his or her physical body. I use this term interchangeably with *ghost* and *earthbound soul*. Being wayward, I believe, is not a good thing.

Introduction

Along with my daughter, Colette, I have been crossing way-wards to the light for well over a decade. (Or, as we often like to call it, "wayward wrangling.") One thing that we have found while doing this work is that when souls go wayward, they stop their spiritual development, for the most part, for the time that they are wayward—whether it is a day or hundreds of years. After the soul gets home, it realizes that it has to make up for the time spent wayward, and also for whatever karma it collected while wayward. Some waywards actively try to disrupt the physical environment around them in negative ways, or maybe even harm the physical people they consider trespassers in their "territory." This is one way that an earthbound soul collects unwanted karma that must be dealt with in a future lifetime. It's bad enough when people do this in their physical lifetime, but to do this after going wayward is just plain stupid. That is why we try to cross these earthbound souls as quickly as we can after finding out about them (although occasionally waywards first need to spend some time with us and learn something, either about themselves or from us).

Overall, crossing waywards is the most rewarding volunteer work I have ever been involved with. My hope is that as well as enjoying the stories I've included, my readers will approach this book as a series of how-to lessons for guiding waywards to the other side … home … heaven … summerland … or whatever you like to call that place where God resides (and where we reside when not living a physical lifetime). Of course, not everyone who reads these stories will want to cross waywards like Colette and I do, but everyone has the ability to reach out a hand and help a lost soul back to the light—simply by lighting a candle and saying, "Go to the light." It may take time, but eventually the push from this side, and the pull from the other side, will get lost souls to where they need to be. I think that this book will be especially useful for those of you who are sensitive enough to feel a ghost around and truly want to help.

That was me, when I became aware of my first wayward.

She was a little girl, around eight or ten years old. I had a dream about her. In the dream, a thunderstorm rolled in after midnight, lightning flashed, and thunder crashed. I went to the window to close the shade, but stopped short as a bolt of lightning lit up the backyard.

A wooden box was on the lawn a few feet from the house, and a young girl with a long blue dress sat on it. Her dark brown hair was pulled back from her face and tied with a ribbon that matched the light blue collar on her old-fashioned dress. She wore black boots that buttoned up the side, to just above her ankles.

The girl looked up. She was completely dry, and not affected by the wind whipping around the yard. I stifled a scream as I saw what seemed to be an evil smile on her face.

"Who are you?" I asked in my dream, and banged my palm against the windowpane.

The child only gazed at me and smiled more broadly.

My stomach clenched painfully and my throat tightened.

"Who are you?"

There was no response … only the smile.

"Who are you?" I screamed as I slammed my hands against the window again and again. "Who are you?" The pane cracked, but I continued banging against the glass. "Who are you?"

The child did not answer, only smiled.

Suddenly it was daylight. The dream-storm was over, and the sun was shining brightly.

I stumbled from my bed and looked at the unbroken window. I ran my finger across the smooth pane, expecting to feel it slice into my skin at any moment, but it didn't; the break in the glass wasn't there in my waking state. I wondered who the little girl was.

The next night I dreamed of her again. She was standing in the kitchen and I was beside her.

"Who are you?"

"My name is Mary Elizabeth Paul."

I stared incredulously at her.

"My daddy hurt me."

"What?"

"He hit me in the head with a big stick."

"When? Where is he? Where is your mommy?"

"He hurt Mommy, too, but she didn't get up; she just went to sleep."

The last thing I heard her say, as I awakened from the dream, was "May 16, 1896."

In the weeks following the dreams, all I wanted to do was help this little girl. She seemed so lost and alone, but I had no idea where to start. I researched death records for the date and name, as well as for anything close to them, but found nothing. A fire had swept through our town around the turn of the century, and most of the courthouse records that contained births and deaths had been destroyed.

Today, when I interpret these two dreams, I think that the thunderstorm was a symbol of the turbulent emotions I would experience over five years later, when I realized that I had made a commitment to helping waywards to the light. The box the girl was sitting on symbolized her "boxed-in" situation—being wayward. The window showed me that although I could see the ghost, there was still a separation; then, when the glass cracked, I was breaking through the barrier that separated us and could communicate with her.

Often, for the rest of the time we lived in the house where I'd had the dreams, my family and I heard things. Occasionally we would hear the kitchen cabinet doors slam. When the kitchen was renovated and new cabinets put in, the doors slammed incessantly for the first three nights. I would get up to see what the problem was, only to find nothing unusual—the doors were all closed, as I had left them before going to bed. When I would look at the clock to see the time, it was usually around three in the morning. This is when one's psychic center is most active.

Other times, I would hear someone playing our piano. Just a few notes, but enough to awaken me completely. I would discover that the piano's lid was still covering the keyboard. Sometimes I would see a wisp out of the corner of my eye, but when I looked directly at it, there would be nothing there. I now believe that all of these things, along with other experiences later on, served to prepare Colette and me for the work we were to do with waywards.

Colette had her own introduction to waywards. A new Wal-Mart was built in our town, and a very old, small, limestone house occupied the land between the huge new building and the road. Colette saw a woman there. I knew there was no one living in the house, but I also knew that Colette was telling the truth about what she saw. She was seeing a ghost—but neither of us knew what to do about it.

We eventually learned that the house was to be razed, and somehow the soul in the house knew it, too. Colette was receiving impressions from the wayward: she didn't want her house torn down, and she wanted Colette to help her. Colette was only ten years old at the time, and there wasn't much she could do for the woman. I was at a loss as well.

The good news is that both of these waywards—the woman from the house and the little girl from my dreams—have crossed over and are now in a much happier place. We learned this years later, path-walking on the subject after we had begun crossing waywards in earnest.

If you have ever had an experience where you saw or felt a ghost and felt the need to help it, even if the incident frightened you, this book is for you. I have heard many people say about their chosen cause in life, "If I can help just one person…" Colette and I don't feel this way—we want to help as many souls as possible; just one isn't going to be enough. I would like to see more people get this attitude. Yes, putting a lot of effort into something just to help one person sounds noble, but if you think logically and are smart about your effort, you could help many. I hope this book will be a call to those of you with the ability to help cross way-wards. Not everyone can see or hear ghosts, but if you think you may have one around, please consult these stories and use them as a kind of instruction manual—a workbook, if you will—on how to guide a lost soul back.

One thing I would like to emphasize, at this point, is to always remember that the spirit memory never forgets. So, when people go to a reputed haunting, for entertainment or financial gain, and demand that ghosts show up for digital cameras or make some sort of physical gesture as "proof" that they exist, the waywards will remember these people if they meet them in another life-time; whatever earthbound souls learn while wayward, they take with them into their next life. There will be resentment (whether conscious or not) from these souls toward those who teased them when they were in need of help…love…understanding. Colette and I find it very difficult when we see or hear about people who do this. As well as adding to the earthbound soul's confusion and grief, it can make them frustrated; when ghosts get frustrated, they become angry. Not a whole lot of people can handle dan-gerous waywards. In general, just remember that at one time, all ghosts were physical human beings. They were someone's mother or father, aunt or uncle, daughter or son, and they all deserve our respect. They are confused individuals who, deep down, just want to go home.

I must add that, along these lines, I don't think there's a prob-lem with capturing the image of a ghost on film or video if it's done respectfully and with the right intention (or by accident).

Having a digital camera handy on a humid day or night, especially when the veil between the physical and psychic worlds is thinnest (around Halloween and Easter), can be helpful in viewing a wayward's form if they choose to allow it. They usually appear rather wispy—like smoke or fog that you can see through, for the most part, or perhaps even as a shadow. Sometimes there are colors visible in the mistiness. Colette and I believe that the "orbs" that sometimes appear in digital pictures are actually spirits, not waywards. (I use the term *spirits* to refer to souls who have crossed and are whole once again.)

As a practicing Wiccan for over twenty-five years, I have been asked if being Wiccan has anything to do with my or my daughter's ability to cross waywards to the light. In a way it does; in a way it doesn't. Wicca has given Colette and me the courage to look into ourselves and know that we have the ability to do this job. And since I perceive Wicca as being about helping others, dedicating myself to helping lost souls seems very appropriate. But Colette and I feel that just about anyone, of any religion, can do this wonderful volunteer work. Everyone has the ability to reach out and offer assistance. We hope we can encourage people to do this, regardless of whether the individual they help exists in the physical or the nonphysical realm. We believe that we have helped both categories of people through our work.

A closing note: all of the stories in this book are true. I have changed the names of most of the physical people involved to protect their privacy. Many of the people mentioned, however, knew that I was writing this book and liked the idea of having their experiences shared, since they felt that their stories could help both physical and nonphysical souls. So, read on, to get a little glimpse into the lives of two women who help those souls whom most people cannot see.

And keep this thought in mind … if they are shadows to us, what are we to them?

Part One

the waywards

The Haunted House on Main Street

"**T**hat beautiful house on Main Street is for rent," I said to my husband as I walked into the townhouse apartment we were renting in 1995. My kids, Colette and Christopher, began clamoring for an after-school snack as they took off their coats and backpacks, but I was still focused on the house. "I'd like to check it out," I continued. "If it's not too much, I wouldn't mind moving there. It's got a big backyard for the kids to play in and there's a playground not too far away."

"Really?" my husband asked, continuing to read the newspaper. "Do you really want to move?"

"I think the kids would enjoy playing in that yard. It's a big backyard."

The house was a beautiful old red brick house with limestone accents on it and a tile roof. It was a typical, modest, turn-of-the-century house. From the outside you could see two chimneys, and I had wanted a house that had a fireplace for over ten years. Before moving to Kentucky, we had lived in a house in Florida with a fireplace, and I had really enjoyed it.

The next day, I convinced my husband to drive by the house and get the telephone number off the *for rent* sign. As it turned out, the real estate office across the street from the house was the place we needed to go. It, too, was a beautiful old home. The wooden clapboard siding was painted a pristine white that made the black wooden shutters stand out magnificently. It was located in the old section of our small town, and the yards of all these houses were well-kept and large, mainly because they were mostly businesses now; the businesses made their large backyards into parking lots for their customers. That is, except for the wonderful brick house and the houses on either side of it, which were still single-family residences.

"I just signed a lease with a young couple a few hours ago," the man in charge of renting said to us. "I really wish y'all had come by first."

I was incredibly disappointed, but I knew that if it was meant to be, we would eventually move into that beautiful old house with the big backyard.

A few months later, in February 1996, the house was up for rent again. This time I went straight to the real estate office.

"Sure," the man said as he gave me the key. "We haven't looked at it yet, though. The people just returned the keys yesterday."

"That's all right," I said as I took the key. "I just want to look inside."

After getting Colette, age ten, and Christopher, age seven, back into my old Subaru station wagon, I maneuvered the car across the busy Main Street and up the drive of my dream house, parking in the turn-about that was near the garage.

The first thing we noticed as we got out of the car on that cold February day was the pile of garbage behind the house. It was at least four feet tall, six feet wide, and reached about ten feet out from the wall of the house. The last tenants had obviously had no garbage pick-up for the four months they'd lived there.

After opening the front door, I stepped back because of the smell that exploded from inside the house. There was a definite odor of rotten food, baby diapers, and animal smells of all kinds, including feces and urine. The house was a total wreck, with week-old food and trash everywhere we looked. Most memorably, we discovered a white rabbit in a small cage on top of the kitchen counter, pawing wildly at the wire that kept it captive. Its water bottle was empty, so I filled it and it lapped the liquid up until the bottle was half empty. I found a half of a sack of potatoes and put one into the cage; the rabbit began to devour it ravenously. (The rabbit eventually went to the humane society because we were all allergic to him. He did find a good home.)

The first floor of the house had beautiful hardwood floors in the living room, formal dining room, and small bedroom. The upstairs, once a walk-in attic, had been converted into three bed-rooms and a bath in the late 1950s, when the electricity had been wired. I loved the way the current owners, the Walton family, had creatively used space in the attic. There were built-in bookcases throughout most of the house, enough for all our books for the first time ever. What would eventually become my son's room had two built-in trundle beds, and the bedroom that my daughter chose had two built-in desks, folding out from the knee walls under the steep ceiling. The closets were huge, even if the slant of the roof affected how tall they were.

Soon, chirping began to attract my attention to the front of the house on the first floor. To the side of the front door was what could only be described as a sunroom, with red industrial tile on the floor and windows wrapping around from the front to the side of the house. There we found a mated pair of zebra finches in a cage, again with no water or food. They got water, but I couldn't find food; the poor little birds were already picking their feathers out because of the stress they were under. It turned out that we were able to keep the finches, and they lived for a couple of years after that.

We then went into the basement, and as I descended the stairs, I was startled by a large black shape flying up into a vent in the ceiling at the base of the staircase.

"Be careful, kids. It looks like there's a bird loose down here."

We explored the cavernous basement. Amid the trash were carcasses from numerous mice, like the ones you would purchase from a pet store, and a few piles of what could only be described as feces. This worried me a little, because it meant the previous tenants had housed snakes or some sort of carnivorous reptiles down here. It didn't look like any snakes were there at that point, nor did it smell like it; it just smelled like a musty basement with shit in it.

But still, overall, I could see the house as a beautiful, warm, and inviting home. I could picture the curtains I would make for the large windows on the first floor, elegant but simple. Our large maple dinette would look great in the breakfast room. Our antique maple bedroom suite would go in the large bedroom on the second floor that faced the backyard.

Little did I realize that renting this house would mark the beginning of a fifteen-month struggle with a very cranky earth-bound soul.

Over the next two weeks, I cleared out garbage and items left by the previous tenants. Scrubbing every inch of the floors and walls as well as having the windows open (for as long as I could stand the cold weather) helped with the smell. I learned not to eat anything for a couple of hours before going to clean, and could not eat anything for a couple of hours afterwards because of the nausea the smell of the garbage caused in me. It took a large tarp lining the entire back of the station wagon (with the back seat down) and about ten trips to the dump before the garbage behind the house was taken care of. After cleaning up this garbage, I discovered the gas meter and a ninety-gallon garbage can, full to overflowing of course. The latter was emptied as soon as we arranged for garbage pick-up. After another four or five trips with the back of my Subaru filled up, all the stuff from inside the house was taken care of as well.

The one really strange thing I found during this massive cleaning project was in the master bedroom closet. It looked as if a makeshift altar had been made from a microwave cart. There were red candles and a few shot glasses on it, one of which had strange symbols on it that I didn't recognize. I eventually discovered the symbols were Hebrew in origin, and were protective. I realized, later, that the previous tenants had felt an overpowering negativity in the house as well.

A few days after we moved in, my husband had to go back to work. He worked the third shift and would be gone all that night, and the next three. I tucked the kids into bed and settled in myself, saying a prayer of thanksgiving for being able to move into such a beautiful house.

Just as I drifted off to sleep, I felt something—or should I say, someone—hitting the bottoms of my feet violently. Scared silly, I sat upright immediately and the beating stopped. A few hours later I was able to get back to sleep. I woke up the next morning feeling somewhat tired, but I attributed this to all the cleaning and moving I had just accomplished.

That morning, after my husband got home from work, I told him about the strange problem I'd had with my feet.

"I'm sure you were just dreaming," he said.

"Yeah, I'm sure that's all it was," I said, not completely convinced.

The next night I again tucked the kids into bed and retired myself. I was again awakened, in the middle of the night, to strange happenings. This time the whole bed was jumping up and down and shaking back and forth.

Jesus! I thought. *What the hell is going on?*

Even after I sat up, the bed continued its gyrating dance. "Scared out of my wits" does not begin to describe how I felt this time. I was also afraid the noise would wake up my children. Frightened or not, I would not allow this demon to disturb my children! Sweat was dripping off my shaking body and my breaths were coming in ragged, fear-induced gasps.

"Stop it and go away!" I whispered loudly.

The undulating stopped. I listened carefully for any sounds from the kids' rooms. All was quiet. I got up and checked in on them both; they had slept through the whole thing. Next, I grabbed a flashlight and searched my entire room, the second floor, and eventually the house, not wanting to turn on the lights because it might wake them up. I found a spare night-light and plugged it in near my bed. It gave off a comforting light; I could see everything in the room well but I would still be able to sleep ... if I could.

I stayed awake for several hours this time. Every little noise and creak frightened me. Even the trees outside my window, groaning under the punishment of the wind, kept my vivid imagination active. I kept the blankets pulled up tightly to my chin and frantically looked around every time the old house made the slightest noise.

I like to be frightened as well as the next person, but in the movie house or watching a scary movie on television—not in my own house as I sleep! Or at least, try to sleep.

Again, I told my husband about what had happened when he was at work. He took me a little more seriously this time, but still tried to attribute it to a bad dream in a new place.

"I wasn't dreaming. I was sitting up when I told the thing to go away. The bed was still shaking! I felt like I was in a bad replay of *The Exorcist!*"

"That's not it," he said, and changed the subject.

A few weeks after we moved in, our next-door neighbor, Gina, offered me a job at the kennel she managed. I loved it! The kennel was a few miles out in the country, among rolling hills. I cleaned the pens and fed the dogs and cats, a pet skunk, a pig, and two goats, and got paid for it. When Gina first hired me, she strongly suggested that I get a dog and bring him with me to work. She said she would feel better if I had a dog to protect me, because sometimes I would be getting through with my work after dark. Since my husband was working nights and the nighttime disturbances at our new house were still occurring, I thought a dog was a fantastic idea. At least I wouldn't feel so lonely, and I knew I would definitely feel safer. Animals have a way of calming you down, and they can sense when someone or something else is around—most of the time better than we can

We found Shiloh, our dog, through a newspaper ad: "free to good home." I called the woman, who wanted references. Gina offered to be a reference, and we brought Shiloh home a few days later. He was about ten weeks old and nothing but a ball of black fur. He was overly friendly to everyone and had a penchant for getting into trouble.

Later that summer, we decided also to adopt Nicky, a full-grown Dalmatian/husky mix who was antisocial with just about everyone except me. He was completely dependent on me within a few weeks and experienced separation anxiety whenever I left the house without him.

Strange things continued to happen around the house. Items would mysteriously disappear. Sometimes we would find them weeks or months later in a different place; that is, if we found them at all. (I "lost" my favorite T-shirt and Colette "lost" a book; neither was ever found.) When we first moved in, we found that we had to replace several lightbulbs that had burned out. That was not unusual, but the three in the light in my bedroom would burn out or explode within a month or two of being replaced. Sometimes one at a time, sometimes two at once; I learned to keep a box of fresh bulbs in my bedroom closet as well as a stepladder. At that point in time, however, I was convinced that the previous tenants had called up a demon and that this demon was the cause of the unexplained happenings I was experiencing.

I read all I could on protection spells in my Wiccan books. I gathered yarrow and bought and grew sage and rosemary, hanging the herbs around and above my bed in the hopes that I could get a good night's sleep. I also smudged the entire house with rosemary or sage smoke, keeping at least one window open for the negativity to escape and trying desperately to drive the negativity out.

That summer passed with only minor incidents. I did occasionally seem to see a big black "bird" hovering in a corner of the kitchen, breakfast room, or bedroom; however, the real problems that first year began after it started getting cold. The heating system in our old house was an ancient boiler in the basement and baseboard heaters throughout the house. I wanted to enjoy the fireplace in the living room (the other fireplace was located in the kitchen and had long ago been made into a wall), so I called local chimney sweeps.

"Does Doug Walton still own this old house?" The chimney sweep asked when he arrived at the house.

"Yes, I believe he's the youngest of the Walton kids," I said.

"Me and him went to school together. We used to have sleepovers at each other's houses," he said, and paused. "You know his mother committed suicide, right?"

"Really?"

Great, I thought. *On top of a demon in my house, we had a woman commit suicide. No wonder this place hasn't had a renter for more than a year or so at a time.*

"Yeah. I was spending the night with Doug and his mom and dad had a fight. She went off to the motel she usually went to when they had fights. In the morning we went to find her. We saw her car in the parking lot, but it had snowed the night before; the car was covered, so we didn't think much of it. When we found out that she hadn't checked in, Mr. Walton went to her car, scraped the snow off, and found her inside. The needle was still in her arm," he said. "She used to be a nurse and was on some kind of pain medicine."

Great. Coincidence? There are no coincidences.

"Yeah, she's buried right out there in the cemetery," he said, pointing in the direction of the town graveyard a few blocks away. "Mr. Walton remarried within a year and died a few years later. Yeah, they're buried next to each other—'As they're married, so they're buried.' They were buried with her on the right and him on the left."

That had been twenty-five years ago. Our next-door neighbors, two old ladies, confirmed the chimney sweep's story and told us about where Mrs. Walton's gravesite was. My daughter and I searched the large cemetery until we found her tombstone. She had died in 1972, her husband in 1978.

One cold day I was startled by what could only be described as an explosion that seemed to come from the basement. I ran downstairs and saw a cloud of white billowing across the top of the ceiling. I called the man at the real estate office, who calmly explained that it was the old boiler venting steam. After that it became somewhat common to hear the boiler's safety valve let off a wave of steam, filling the basement with the hot fog.

Several times that winter we had problems with the heat. One floor would be eighty-five degrees and the other two would be fifty-two degrees. There was only one person in the area who was licensed to work on the antique boiler, and it would sometimes be days before he could come over. When he did make it to the house, invariably he would find nothing wrong, but tried his best by replacing parts that could have been the culprit. The heating problems continued throughout the cold months. We got to know Phil, the boiler repairman, quite well.

Spring came finally, and my nerves were more frazzled than ever. The boiler "exploded" two or three times a month, and the lightbulbs in our bedroom were costing us a small fortune. I was having bad dreams as well, mainly about things chasing me or trying to get me. In one dream I still vividly remember, I was lying in bed. Above me were pipes, old and rusty and covered in some sort of nasty-looking brown goo. I started to get out of bed, but found I couldn't move. I watched as the goo began to ooze out— it looked like it was going to drop right onto my face! Then I felt someone's hand on my chin, pulling my mouth open so that the goo would drop down my throat. I jerked my hand up, swatting at my chin, and I actually felt my hand knock something away from my face.

Enough was enough. I had just replaced my old protective herbs with fresh ones, but things weren't improving. I decided to call the local Catholic church to see if they could perform an exorcism on the house. After replacing the lightbulbs in my bedroom … again … I started down the stairs to make the call.

I felt a push from behind me, and let out a startled gasp as I fell down the stairs. Instinctively I grabbed the flimsy handrail, praying it would hold, and held on for dear life. I finally stopped my downward decent, but my back was hurt and it felt like my shoulder was sprained with the effort of holding onto the banister. Nicky came up to me and tried to put his large head under my arm, as if to help me up. Right then I was extremely grateful he was such a large dog. He helped me as I hobbled downstairs for ice.

Later that day, I called the church and explained I thought I had a demon in my house.

"Are you Catholic?" was the first question the woman asked after I briefly explained what I was experiencing.

"Yes. I was baptized into the faith at two weeks old and confirmed when I was eight years old, but I haven't been to church in a long time."

"So you don't belong to any parish."

"No," I admitted.

"You don't have a demon in your house," the cranky old woman said. "Besides, there are probably only six exorcisms performed each year in the United States."

There was a click and a dial tone.

It was so wonderful to know that the local Catholics were so understanding of spiritual matters! They claimed to help those in need, but you had to be Catholic, first and foremost, and tithed to a particular parish for them to help.

About that time there was a psychic fair at a hotel in Lexington—the same hotel where Mrs. Walton had committed suicide—and I decided to go. I needed juniper berries. I'd found an exorcism ritual in one of my books and planned on using it on the demon, and juniper berries were the one ingredient I had yet to get to make the spell work. The kids wanted to go, so we'd have some fun looking at all the neat stuff, and I could get what I needed to get rid of what I didn't need.

I never realized how difficult it is to find juniper berries. I was just about to give up as I went up to the last booth at the fair.

"I'm looking for juniper berries," I said to the woman sitting near the table. "Do you have any?"

"What do you need them for?" The woman asked. She seemed a little older than I was and had long, black hair and dark brown eyes.

The kids were still very young and I didn't feel comfortable allowing them to roam around, so I distracted Colette with the next booth, showing her the crystals there. I held Christopher on my lap as I sat in the chair the woman had offered me.

"I have a demon in my house," I said softly, putting my hands over Christopher's ears. "It's driving me crazy and I don't want it to hurt my children."

"We can help you out. I'm a Cherokee medicine woman, and my friend, who's doing a card reading at that table, is Wiccan. We can take care of your problem for you."

I nodded in acknowledgement at the older, stocky woman doing the card reading. But the way I looked at the medicine woman must have indicated my thoughts about how much money were they going to try to get out of me.

"Of course, we won't charge you any money."

"Well, I could at least fix you dinner or something."

"We do accept dinner for our work!" She laughed, introduced me to her friend, and we all exchanged telephone numbers.

Both women agreed that I needed to get rid of anything the previous tenants had left behind. One thing was a rather large shelf unit that my husband was now using out in the garage to store a few of his tools. I moved all the tools to a safe place in the basement and dismantled the unit. I asked Gina if I could dump the furniture in the kennel Dumpster and she said yes. By now I had sold the Subaru and had a Volvo station wagon, which I drove out to the kennel with the shelf unit. I got there and backed up to the gate that led to the Dumpster, parked the car, and turned off the engine. The gate was locked from the inside, so I went through the building to open the gate. To my astonishment, my car was now gone!

I looked around frantically. Down the hill, wedged against a small tree and a split-rail fence, was my car. It had rolled down the hill, over a small rock wall, and slammed into the tree, then into the fence.

I don't know that much about automatic transmissions, but I didn't think this was a mere accident. I had put the car in park, but when I got into it to extricate it from the tree, fence, and rocks, it was in reverse. I'd always put my standard-shift Subaru in gear when parking on a hill, and it was always there when I came back to retrieve it.

After backing the car up the drive to the Dumpster, I got out and unloaded the junk in the back.

A week went by, and I heard nothing from the medicine woman and her friend. I was beginning to think they had been stringing me along—placating a hysterical woman, then brushing her off. I called and left a message for the medicine woman, saying I was still having problems and briefly explaining about the car. After I got off the phone with her answering machine, I went upstairs and told my husband, who was in the bathroom, that I was losing hope I would ever be rid of this demon! He basically said, "There, there, everything will be all right," and went on with his bath.

The telephone rang. After greeting the man on the other end of the line and telling him that my husband was busy, I began to hear Shiloh, still upstairs, barking madly. I looked to the top of the stairs to see Shiloh barking, his tail tucked between his legs. I'd never seen his tail between his legs before and felt somewhat alarmed. It was then that he came bounding down the stairs at break-neck speed. He looked at me, barked once, then ran back up the stairs and around the corner, barking the whole time.

After quickly getting off the phone, I ran upstairs and tried to calm my puppy down. He was at the door to our bedroom, shaking like a leaf. His hackles were raised all the way down his back! My husband was just getting out of the bathtub and asking what was wrong.

"I'm so tired of this demon!" I exclaimed, stroking my terrified puppy.

A few minutes later the phone rang again. It was the Cherokee medicine woman. I told her what had just happened, and she said she would be over at the next full moon, in a little less than a week. She told me to clean the house thoroughly with rosemary water, buy four rosemary plants, and try to stay as calm as I could.

The night of the full moon arrived and so did the medicine woman and her Wiccan friend. I helped them unload a large drum. They each carried a small cloth sack as well.

The medicine woman instructed me to plant the rosemary plants around the base of the house, keeping them alive as long as I could in the Kentucky weather. If one died, I was to replace it as quickly as possible. (In Native American lore, she explained, sharp sticks were usually placed at the cardinal points around the house to protect against negativity, but since we had small children, she felt that the rosemary plants would be safer and work just as well.)

Inside the house, the medicine woman opened her small cloth bag. She took out a cigar and began to smoke it. "Tobacco is sacred and will help clear the negative energies," she said. "It also carries our prayers to the Great Spirit, especially prayers for protection."

Next, I told the two ladies about the suicide of the previous owner, not really sure why I felt compelled to do so.

"Why are you telling her about Mrs. Walton?" My husband asked.

"That's all right," the Wiccan lady said. "We need to know. She is the one who is causing all your problems."

"But she died in Lexington," I protested.

"But this was her home, and she is drawn back to it," the woman told me as she put a large wooden rosary around her neck.

The three of us—the Wiccan, the medicine woman, and I— went upstairs, to where I had the most trouble with things that went bump in the night.

"Nicky likes to sleep in this corner," I said, showing them a corner of the room where a vent of some sort had always been.

"He gives her solace," the Wiccan lady said. "I see that you've hung sage around this room. The one you hung in that corner is black instead of gray."

I looked closely at the clump of herbs and nodded, noticing for the first time the blackness of the dried leaves, which should have been a pearly gray instead.

"That shows that the sage was working. It was drawing in the negativity that she produces. When we're finished, you'll need to burn all these herbs and bury the ashes where they won't be disturbed."

I nodded as we set the drum beside the bed. The medicine woman handed me a drumstick.

"What am I supposed to do?" I asked.

"Whatever you feel like doing," she answered, and started beating slowly on the hide that stretched across the wooden frame of the drum.

I took a few tentative smacks as the Wiccan lady began praying for the earthbound soul of Mrs. Walton to go to the light.

"We always want to tell the lost one to go to the light, not the other place," the Wiccan woman said over the drum. "Always to the light."

The drum vibrated loudly and desperately as we began beating it faster. After that, we became in sync with one another and the pounding, pulsing vibration filled the room.

"Go, go, go," I began to chant softly, not knowing what else to do or say.

"Please, Mrs. Walton, God loves you and wants you to be with him again," the Wiccan lady was saying loudly, now. "Go to the light. It is where you belong now that your physical body is gone. Go to the light and be at peace!"

A trancelike state overtook us. The chanting of prayers and drumming continued for several minutes. Suddenly I saw a beautiful, white light form before me, with a woman silhouetted in front of it. She had collar-length curly hair, in the 1970s style. She seemed to be staring at me. Then she slowly turned and disappeared into the light.

"She's gone," the Wiccan lady said.

All I could do was stare at her, tears in my eyes. I had seen it happen, and right afterward the Wiccan lady had confirmed it! Wow!

The rest of the time we lived in that lovely brick house, the lightbulbs in the bedroom didn't burn out. The next winter we had no problems with the heating system. No one pushed me down the stairs again, and we didn't lose half as many items as before. It was so nice to be rid of a menacing ghost forever!

But life has a funny way of directing us. Little did I realize that this was just the beginning ....

Afterword

I want to emphasize that I had absolutely no idea what was going on, or what I was doing, during or before the crossing of Mrs. Walton. Obviously the drumming and chanting helped us achieve an altered, trancelike state, which helped us connect with our higher selves and enabled us to better direct, push—whatever—Mrs. Walton to the other side. At the time, I didn't try to think much about the "hows" or "whys" of crossing my first wayward; I was just so incredibly relieved that she was gone!

For several days afterward I was rather weak. I attributed this to putting so much energy into getting Mrs. Walton crossed. During this time I also had the strange experience of people smiling at me and greeting me. People I didn't know. These people seemed to notice that something around them was different. They would look about and then focus on me. The only thing that comes to mind is that I was so happily relieved that I didn't have to put up with an incredibly cranky ghost anymore that my joy at being rid of her was felt by people sensitive enough to pick up on it.

In retrospect, I think it was more my desire and determination to have Mrs. Walton out of my life that was the determining factor in her crossing to the other side. The medicine woman and the Wiccan woman taught me that it also takes a tremendous amount of love to guide a lost soul to the light.

Also, I was in the right frame of mind for this crossing because I had done so much prep work by ridding myself of the last of the things the previous tenants had left and giving the house another very thorough cleaning with rosemary water. Rosemary and sage are very powerful cleansing agents when it comes to negativity.

Commitments

"No, I won't do it," I said as I threw a stick into the fire. I was sitting beside a campfire in a small clearing. There was a man in blue jeans, brown-suede boots, and a blue dungaree shirt squatting beside the fire, opposite where I was. He had brown hair and a placid look on his face. In the firelight, he almost looked like he was glowing. There was a definite orange cast on everything around us.

"I won't do it!" I exclaimed as I got up and began pacing; my argumentative state was having no effect on my calm companion.

The man just let me rant and pace beside the fire. It was dark out, but I could see trees around. We were in a forest and there was a hill behind the man. He stood, picked up three blankets I had not noticed before, and offered them to me. I glared at him as I accepted his gift. Somehow I knew I had to do this. He pointed up the hill and I followed his silent directions.

There was a cave entrance about halfway up, and I went inside. Even though it was dark, somehow I could see. To my left there was a sort of room with several people inside; the area had bars in front of it. It looked like a makeshift prison. The people behind the bars were quiet, not saying a word; just milling around, looking lost and depressed.

I felt compassion for them, and pushed the three blankets, one by one, through the bars. One by one, the people who took the blankets disappeared.

Opening my eyes, I realized I had been dreaming. It was one of those dreams that seem so real … like you're actually living it.

It was fall in Kentucky, 1998. My feet froze solid as soon as they touched the arctic lake of red industrial tile on my bedroom floor. My slippers should have been right where my feet fell, but they had mysteriously disappeared. I knew exactly where to look for them—my puppy, Shiloh, was two years old at this point and loved crawling under my bed at night to sleep. He had pulled my slippers with him, but didn't bring them back out when he crawled out to greet me.

"Damn it, Puppy, I wish you'd leave my slippers where I put them," I said as I rubbed his shaggy black head.

He just wagged his good-morning tail at me and shook himself. Shiloh had grown into a seventy-five-pound Newfoundland with what looked like a little greyhound mixed in. Nicky, who was full-grown when we adopted him, weighed in at around sixty pounds. He wagged his thick, white-tipped black tail, but remained lying on his insulated doggy bed.

After digging my slippers out from the puppy's sleeping quarters and putting them on my cold-as-fish feet, I put my heavy robe on and went down our well-worn pine staircase. Now that Mrs. Walton had gone to the light, no one would ever suspect that our house had housed a negative and spiteful ghost for twenty-five years. The experience with Mrs. Walton during those first fifteen months had nearly driven me to an insane asylum.

In one of the downstairs bookcases was a dream dictionary I trusted: *Mary Summer Rain on Dreams*. I took it to the table with me, fixed myself some toast and hot tea, and tried to remember as many details about the dream as I could. The first person to receive a blanket, in the cave, was a black man; he had been in a tattered shirt with no sleeves and well-worn pants that went down to just below his knees. The next two had been women. The first woman had on a late-1800s-style dress. The third came from the very back of the cave and I couldn't really make out what she was wearing other than that it was a very fitted black dress that came just below her knees. Who were these people, and why were they in a makeshift prison?

My mind kept going back to the man by the campfire. He was beautiful. He seemed to be around thirty years old, and irritatingly sure that I would accept the blankets and follow his silent directions. His demeanor still irritated me! I also had felt calm, almost comforted, after I'd delivered the blankets. For a split second at the end of the dream, I'd felt … emptiness. Like I could have done more for the other people, but didn't. Or was it guilt that I'd felt? I needed to think about this dream more; it seemed important. Then I laughed at myself. The man obviously knew me well, because he knew I would take the blankets and do what needed to be done.

Since most of the time I dream in black and white, the fact that the dream was in color made me take special interest. I was sure it was a message from the other side; I just had to figure it out. It was hard. I was still quite new to psychic stuff, as this recent surge I'd been having lately was unlike anything I'd previously experienced. I'd had dreams and feelings before that I'd followed, and was glad I had, but this seemed different.

A few weeks before, I'd had a vision when I was wide awake. I was looking out the dining room window, and the clouds turned into a giant phoenix that looked directly at me. Ever since then, things had changed … slowly … but they had changed. My dreams started coming in color every now and then; I had strange promptings that turned out to be right; I could touch an object and get impressions from it sometimes.

After thinking about all this for a few minutes, I flipped the pages of the dream dictionary to the left (which meant going in a different direction). I looked up *cave*. *Cave* was said to symbolize instinctively knowing something of value. *Jail* meant jail, losing your freedom—reasonable enough. *Prison* symbolized the same thing; it was just that you imprisoned yourself. I suddenly thought of a dream I'd had when I was a young child.

I was in an asylum-green room, by myself. There was no furniture, no pictures on the walls, and no doorknob on the door— just a hole where one should have been. I was locked in without any way of getting out. I kept hearing people outside the room. It sounded like they were playing some type of game. There was laughter and conversation, but I couldn't make out what was going on. I just wanted to join in and have fun as well. I remember how alone and isolated I felt.

"Grandma? Grandma! I'm in here and I can't get out!"

I just knew Grandma would come to get me soon and give me Chips Ahoy! cookies, my perennial favorite, and milk.

"Grandma, please let me out. I want to go home. I want to go to your house."

Grandma came and let me out at the end of the dream. I remember waking up frightened and shaking.

This must be how ghosts feel: to exist, but to have no one notice them or talk to them. A very lonely feeling.

I was beginning to understand my dream. The people in the cave behind the prison bars were ghosts—waywards, as I now thought of them. I had given a blanket to three of them, even though there were several more there. A blanket would be comfort. Then it dawned on me: was I supposed to help these ghosts to the light? The responsibility of that thought overwhelmed me. How was I supposed to do this? What if something went wrong? After my experiences with Mrs. Walton, I knew that waywards could harm physical people. This could prove to be dangerous work, and I didn't want to hurt myself or anyone else in the process.

I started thinking deeper. If the man in my dream was my spirit guide, then he was letting me know that I had made a commitment, before I came into this physical life, to get three waywards back home. All three had died before I was born. Now my guide was letting me know that it was time to accept my responsibilities and do what needed to be done.

I'd read about reincarnation and how we plan our lives very carefully before we are born into the physical world. What I'd read all seemed very logical to me; it also explained some of the strange dreams I'd had. When I read in Sylvia Browne's book that we plan our lives in a classroomlike setting with books, charts, and maps, I knew it was true because I'd had a dream a few years earlier that I hadn't understood until reading those passages. In my dream, I was in a white room with the man in my most recent dream. We were both dressed in white robes with white, cotton-looking rope tied around our waists. There were maps in blue and gold on the wall, of the United States and the world, with blue lines dissecting them, like travel plans. At the time I'd had the dream I didn't understand it, but after I read Browne's books about the other side, I did.

But how could I even be so egotistical as to think I could actually help lost souls back to where we all came from? Helping to cross one ghost, however mean and spiteful she'd been, was one thing. I'd had the help of a couple of people who had done it before. Now I realized that I had committed to crossing three waywards to the other side, and I didn't see anyone around who could help me with this unconventional task. The Wiccan lady and the medicine woman lived too far away for me to ask them to help me with all three of my commitments. I also didn't know when I was supposed to cross the waywards, or where I would meet them. But I was pretty sure it was going to happen. Given my belief that coincidences are not coincidental, but rather a spiritual smack upside the head, I was sure I'd come to the right conclusion.

Soon, I would know for certain. A couple of days later I took a snack to Colette's drama class, where she was rehearsing a production of *The Frog Prince*. Jane, the teacher, was very easygoing. She was a very light-skinned woman who was slightly older than I was. She had thick glasses, and one of her very light blue eyes wandered. She almost looked like an albino. We were chatting, something I had come to look forward at the drama club meetings, when I noticed that she was looking at the necklace I had on.

"Is that—?"

"It's nothing," I whispered quickly, tucking the pentacle back into my T-shirt and looking around quickly to see if any of the kids had noticed. None had.

Jane grabbed my arm and pulled me out into the hallway, away from the children. Neither of us wanted them to hear what we were talking about. There is still a lot of stigma attached to Wicca and being a witch, especially in the middle of the Bible belt.

"Are you Wiccan?" she asked softly.

"Yes," I said. What else could I say? "I've been studying it since 1982."

"Look," she said, as she checked in on the well-behaved class and dragged me a little farther down the hall. "My son Jacob got this book and tried to call something to him. Now it comes in the house and it's scaring him. I've seen the television turn off and on by itself. Can you help us?"

Damn spiritual smack-upside-my-head!

I stood paralyzed for a moment. What was I going to tell her? I considered Jane a friend, but this was getting pretty personal. Until now I had never spoken to her or anyone else in town about my spiritual beliefs. At the same time, she seemed to be into New Age stuff at least a little bit. Then there was the dream I'd had about the cave. *There are no coincidences...*

"I can try to help you." *Who said that?*

"Thank you so much, Anson! I can pay you."

"I won't accept payment for this kind of stuff. When God starts charging me for the information he gives me, then I'll start charging people for helping them with ghosts. Can you tell me any more about what's going on?"

Jane wasn't able to tell me a lot more, but she did allow me to speak to her son at the next drama club meeting. I had never met him before and was a little surprised that he was so tall at fifteen years old. He had to be at least 5'8" already. He had glasses and dark hair, and was already getting into the goth look by dressing in black pants and a black AC/DC T-shirt.

He'd found a book in the New Age section of a local bookstore and tried to follow a spell in it. He said it was supposed to open his psychic center and allow him to communicate with spirits. (This was my first hint that he might like having a ghost around, even if initially it scared him.) But if you open yourself up psychically, you need to be ready for the consequences. There are a lot of other dimensions besides the physical one, and if you're not prepared for this or don't have someone to help guide you through it, it can be very frightening.

That night I prayed for help. I had a dream, also in color, about a black family at a picnic. There was a mother, two sisters, and a male cousin. I can't explain how I knew who they were, but I did. They all wanted me to bring a young man to them. They called him Nimbi. I got the impression that I was not to mention the word "home" to him, just that his family wanted him with them. The dream scene then changed to what looked like an old plantation somewhere in a flat part of Tennessee, then to a wooded area, among other things. The images came so fast I wondered if I could remember all of them for Jane.

Jane and I discussed all this at the next drama class meeting. I told her that I'd had a dream about her ghost and that his name was Nimbi.

"I got the impression that I was not to tell this young man that he was to go home," I said. "Like 'home' for him was this plantation. I think he was a slave and he ran away, made it as far as the area where your property is now, and died."

"Sounds reasonable," she said. "Yeah, I think you're right. Jacob did tell me that he thought an African American man was standing in the doorway to his bedroom once. Having someone he didn't know in his bedroom really scared him."

I could feel her fear at having an intruder in her house, someone who could come and go as he pleased. Not knowing if he would harm her family. Obviously, he just wanted to have someone acknowledge he was there so he wouldn't be lonely.

"Did they shave the slaves' heads back then?" I asked suddenly.

"I think they did. It was probably to avoid lice."

"I had a flash in my dream of a man with a bald head at the plantation, but in the woods he had short dreadlocks."

"He wouldn't have been able to cut his hair after he escaped from the plantation," she said thoughtfully. "I'm kind of surprised he made it this far north."

"He was determined to get to freedom. I can't blame him for preferring death over slavery."

"Yeah."

We were both quiet for a while, wrapped up in our own thoughts about the situation.

"So, do you think that he knows he's dead?"

"Probably not," I said.

"Wouldn't he realize that he hasn't eaten or drunk anything in a very long time?"

"We create our own realities," I explained. "The drug abuser doesn't believe he's addicted to drugs. When you have a car accident, you can't believe it happened to you; you didn't believe it would ever happen to you."

Jane was silent, and then said, "You know, there are woods all around my house. I live by the river."

"The river runs that close to your property?"

"Oh yeah, the Kentucky River twists and turns all over this state. He could find water, and there's plenty of game around that he would have been able to hunt and eat."

"Plus all the edible plants in the area."

"Jacob and I will help any way we can," Jane offered after a moment, volunteering her child's cooperation as only a mother can.

"Good," I said. "I'm going to need all the help I can get to get this guy crossed over."

After Colette and I got home that night, I asked both of my children if they wanted to help. Both agreed. They thought it would be fun; I was a basket case.

A week or so later, it was the full moon, just like when the Wiccan lady and the medicine woman had helped me cross Mrs.

Walton. I figured that if it was good enough for them, it would be good enough for me. I packed the kids into the station wagon and we followed Jane's directions to her house.

I was surprised that the wooded area around Jane's house was so much like what I had seen in my dream; I had been given good information. Tall pine, oak, and maple trees were scattered among the undergrowth. Jane's long and rutted driveway was made of rock and dirt that twisted between trees and small gullies all the way up to her house. The house was crouched at the base of a hill, like a wildcat ready to pounce on unwelcome guests. I could feel a lot of positive energy around us and I began to feel confident that we could cross this wayward. I even felt the presence of my grandfather, who had passed away several years earlier, with me. That comforted me more than anything else.

Before we tried to cross Jacob's wayward, we had a short meditation and prayer time together. I sat quietly in an overstuffed chair in Jane's living room and calmed my mind for several minutes. I wasn't sure I was doing the meditation thing right, but I followed my instincts, nebulous as they were, about what I needed to do.

"Please, God, help me...help us to lead Nimbi back to you, where he will find peace and love in your arms. Please help him to understand that we only want what is best for him, and that is to be back where he belongs, where we all belong, home with you," I prayed.

Then we all went out into the woods in front of Jane's house. We were dressed in jeans and T-shirts with jackets, Jacob in black, as usual.

"There's a lot of poison ivy around here, kids, be careful," I said, knowing we were all highly allergic to the oils from the plant.

"You're protected," Jane said confidently, and I looked at her with a silent question. "You're doing God's work. You won't get hurt."

I nodded in agreement. I could feel the truth of her statement throughout my body as goose bumps flooded over my skin. We continued walking around her large, wooded front yard.

At one point I had a vision of a skeleton curled up on the ground. Whenever my children or I have visions it's not like it is in the movies or on television. We don't get a headache suddenly, or stop dramatically, blinking and swaying and acting like we're going to fall down. It's just like seeing a movie or snapshots in your head. Sometimes the visions can be so intense that I see just the vision and none of the surrounding landscape. Sometimes, in these situations, I think it's real for a few seconds because it's so intense. But for the most part, I know that these visions are data from the other side, and accept it as such.

"I think he died here," I said, pointing to the ground. "I see a human skeleton in this little depression by this rock."

The human skeleton I saw was superimposed on the ground. I could see through it, to the ground underneath it.

"He probably died of exposure or hunger," Jane said as she looked at the ground near my feet. "Do you feel him around?"

"Yeah, but he's keeping his distance. He's scared."

I'm sure the wayward had a certain mistrust of me, since I'm white, but he trusted Jacob, even though Jacob was white as well. I assumed that it had something to do with them being around the same age, and the fact that Jacob had sought him out in a way. I directed Jacob to help draw Nimbi to us.

We could periodically hear twigs snapping, as if someone was walking near us, and occasionally a bush or tree branches moved as Nimbi trekked around us. We tried for half an hour to cross him, but he just wouldn't go. I was becoming frustrated. And then it finally occurred to me what the problem was.

"Jacob," I said quietly, my determination outpacing my frustration. "He won't go home if you don't want him to."

I could see that Jacob was surprised at my the truth of my statement. He now wanted Nimbi to stay with him, not go home.

"You have to want him to go, Jacob," his mother said.

"I'm sorry, but you can't have a 'pet wayward,'" I said gently. "It's not fair to him. You've had a nice visit with him, but now it's time for him to go where he needs to go." (Little did I know that we would eventually find our own pet wayward a few years later…)

"You're right," he finally said. "I just want him to be happy and with his family."

"That's the right attitude to have."

After that, it was relatively easy. The five of us crossed Nimbi, the first wayward I had committed to. We formed a circle and began saying an impromptu prayer for him to see the light and to go to it.

"Nimbi, we know you are alone and frightened," I began, trying hard to put my feelings and thoughts into words. "Your family is on the other side of the light and they want you to be with them. They are happy there and want to share their happiness with you."

"You need to go to your family, Nimbi," Jane added. "They have missed you for a very long time. They love you very much and want you to be happy with them."

We raised enough energy that the tunnel of light opened above our heads.

"I see the tunnel above us," I said, "but Nimbi isn't going through it."

"I feel that we need to push him up," Jane said. "He just needs a little push to get him started."

So we pushed Nimbi up into the tunnel. How? I'm not sure, other than through our desire and determination to get him to where we knew happiness and love existed for him.

We went back to Jane's house, where she showed me her throwing wheel and the pottery she had made on it.

"Please, pick something out; I feel I owe you something."

"You really don't owe me anything," I said. "This is something that needed to be done and we did it."

"Just pick out something."

She did make some nice pottery, and I chose a large iridescent black coffee mug. I kept it for years until my dog Nicky knocked it off a counter and broke it. Jane also gave me a votive candleholder that I still have and keep very dear to my heart.

I was pleased and relieved as we drove back home. Although I didn't feel as drained or elated as when I helped cross Mrs. Walton, I still felt peaceful and calm. My grandpa must have gone back home with Nimbi, because I no longer felt his presence. In the days that followed, I kept checking my children and myself, but none of us had any signs of poison ivy from traipsing through the underbrush in Jane's front yard. I kept telling myself that I only had two more waywards to go, and my commitments would be satisfied. I wanted to hurry up and find the remaining two and cross them over so I could get back to my life.

But life has a funny way of directing us, sometimes. This turned out to be just the beginning. I didn't know how many ghosts were around me, but I eventually got a good idea of it and tried to cross as many as I could. Colette felt the same way.

I didn't meet the next ghost from my commitment dream until two years later, after I'd learned a bit more about the art of crossing waywards. We dubbed her Marcella, and she was quite stubborn. We figured she died in the late 1800s. I'm not sure how she died, but that doesn't always matter. (The name of the wayward doesn't always matter either, but it was helpful to me to know, during those first few years of this odd work.) I kept seeing an old-fashioned house under construction. Marcella seemed to be waiting for her house to be renovated. I dressed in overalls and tucked my hair up under an old hat and parked on the road near where she "lived."

Marcella lived on private property, and we knew the people who physically lived there. Colette had been friends with the girls, but for some reason, still unknown to us, we were abruptly told that Colette was not to call the girls anymore, nor was she welcome in their house. I wasn't going to trespass on my daughter's former friends' property, but I was determined to keep my commitment to crossing this wayward. So I acted like I was taking a walk up and down the road. I stayed on the sidewalk, just beyond their property.

For at least twenty minutes, as Colette waited in the van, I argued with Marcella, telling her that I was a worker from her new house and that the renovations on it were finished. She could go home any time she wanted, but now would be a good time. I could even escort her there.

"See," I said after she had begun to follow me, "they even left the lights on for you."

"I don't see any lights," she quipped.

Stubborn-assed wayward. That's why she's been here for so long!

"Yes, ma'am, right ahead of us."

I felt queasy in my solar plexus and wondered if something was wrong. Would she cross? I decided to ignore the nausea and continue onward, and it worked! The queasiness became profound when I walked through the light, but at least Marcella followed, going home at last. Even though I spent some time crossing Marcella, the police were never called. I was beginning to feel that Jane was right; we were protected while doing God's work.

When I got back into the van, I told Colette about the sensations I'd felt. We decided to find out what that was all about.

As it turned out, our spirit guides confirmed that it was a natural thing for me to feel homesick when I was near or walked through a tunnel of light. I just wanted to go back home where my spirit knew I belonged, but for now I had work to do on this earthly plane and would remain in the physical world until my time to go home came. My guide had better have his running shoes on, because I'm not going to waste any time going to the light!

Afterword

Nimbi was the first wayward I crossed without help from more experienced people. I wasn't at all sure I could do this; in fact, I was terrified that I would not be able to help Jane. At the same time, I felt compelled to try. If it worked, then I would know that I was doing what I was supposed to be doing.

One thing I'd like to point out is the importance of preparing yourself, mentally and emotionally, before you conduct a crossing. As I described, after we arrived at Jane's house, I sat in one of her overstuffed chairs and began to meditate. I prayed that all would go well with this crossing. I calmed my mind and began some breathing techniques. I visualized that I was deeply inhaling pure white light, held my breath for a few seconds to allow it to seep throughout my body, and exhaled any negativity within me, visualizing it as dark gray or black smoke coming out of my mouth. This helped to raise my spiritual vibrations and prepare me for crossing Nimbi.

This was a group crossing, of course, where there were several physical people involved in helping the wayward to go home. Every situation is different, but I think the group was important in this case because each of us needed to learn something from helping Nimbi. I had to gain confidence in myself and my abilities, and see that I could do this work without the help of a more experienced person. I also learned that I would not have committed to something that I didn't have the strength, desire, and determination to complete.

Jacob needed to learn to let go of someone he knew didn't belong with him. Even though Nimbi was lonely after having been wayward for so long, and had found a friend in Jacob, we first had to convince Jacob that crossing Nimbi was the right thing to do. Once Jacob understood this, Nimbi realized that Jacob had only his best interests at heart, and he crossed. This was a very valuable lesson for Jacob to learn, and we were very proud of one so young for learning this lesson in love.

Jane needed to learn that not all things that go bump in the night are evil or malevolent; most of the time, things that frighten us aren't so bad when the light of love is shined upon them. My children needed to learn that they weren't alone when it came to sensing things that other people didn't. They realized they weren't crazy; that their gifts were from God, and they needed to use them for the good of those around them, even if those people were already physically dead. Of course, I needed to learn all of these things for myself as well.

You may be wondering why Nimbi didn't cross right after he died. I believe that fear was his problem. In my experience, fear is one of the biggest reasons why someone goes wayward, and it can manifest in so many different ways. In this case, Nimbi thought that going home meant going back to the plantation where he'd been a slave; that's why we couldn't tell him to go home.

Colette and I crossed a wayward within a group situation only one other time. This ghost also was fearful about crossing. She had been murdered and didn't want to see her killers again (it turned out that there wasn't a problem with this, because her killers were still in the physical world). Even though both Colette and I knew that either one of us, alone or together, could guide this lost soul back home, we asked others to participate because we believed that this earthbound soul was meant to be an introduction to teaching wayward wrangling. Afterwards, however, most of those who participated felt that they had done their good deed, and that was the end of their involvement. I realized later that there was too much jealousy and envy in this group for us to teach them much of anything. But this is what free-will choice is all about—the group had the choice to learn to help waywards to cross over, or not. While I don't condone shirking one's responsibility or turning away from someone who needs help, I respect the choices made by the individuals involved. When Colette and I do find individuals who want to commit to this path, we work with them so that they can see that their potential is real and they can do it.

At this time, Colette and I truly saw our potential in helping to guide ghosts back home. With the help of the other side and our spirit guides, we learned, and are still learning, to help those earthbound souls back to the light, to the peace and love that exist there for all of us.

In this book, I often refer to my *spirit guides*. These are souls we have made a contract with, who help us keep to our path in this physical lifetime. Usually they have had at least one incarnation on this dark rock. These individuals are usually friends to us, but they are not too close. They need to have a certain distance from us, so that we can fall down and learn to get back up by ourselves. Colette and I are too close to guide each other; therefore, before we reincarnated, we choose to come down into the physical world together. In past lives we have been parent and child, siblings, cousins, and friends.

My main guide in this lifetime is a rather big guy named Akala. He and I made an agreement that I was to figure things out on my own, for the most part. I believe this is so my psychic abilities will continue to grow. At times this has been frustrating, but I know in my heart that I would never have it any other way.

Akala and I have had at least one past life together that I know of. We were married. We were pagan in that lifetime, in Germany, and I was burned at the stake for being a witch while he was forced to watch. He has assured me that I will not burn for being a witch in this lifetime.

The ghosts that Colette and I committed to cross, when we were planning this physical lifetime, went wayward before we were born, and died before we were born. They will all be crossed by the time we come to the end of our physical lives. But we have chosen to help others as well, who have gone wayward after we were born. For me, Mrs. Walton was one of these souls. There are numerous other waywards (some of whom I have written about in this book) that we helped that we didn't have to. That's just the way we are. When we see someone in need, and we have the means to help, we help. Learning all about love is the whole point of being in the physical world. If we can learn to love one another under these difficult circumstances on this dark rock we call Earth, then we achieve true spiritual advancement and become closer to God. I believe that there is a Mother God and a Father God—Mom and Dad, as I call them. It makes sense. When you look at nature, there is a male and female of every creature and in every plant.

It is important to understand that for a lost soul, being earthbound is like putting your life on hold. When a soul is in this kind of spiritual limbo, no learning can take place. It's a waste of the soul's time to be wayward. Yes, we have eternity to perfect ourselves, but does anyone want to waste time in a self-imposed purgatory if he doesn't have to?

Our Pet Wayward

"**M**an, this storm is something else!" I exclaimed as I drove down our narrow road, which curved dangerously into sudden drop-offs. My husband and I had been trying to make it home before the storm got bad, but it didn't work. "It's like a cow peeing on a flat rock!"

The wind suddenly picked up to a ferocious level. The deafening sound was accompanied by heavy rain, and I pulled the van to the side of the road. There were tall trees on either side of the road here, so we were somewhat protected. We were only about a half-mile from our new house, but I felt it would be better if I didn't drive in this blinding rain. Strong gusts of wind had us rocking back and forth, in what we would later learn was a mid-November tornado.

After the wind and rain lessened a little, we continued home. We had left Colette there, and I was a little worried about how she'd fared. (Christopher was attending an after-school event, so wasn't affected by the tornado.) Colette was fine, just a little shaken because she'd seen the tornado form, down the hill, and watched it as it came toward the house. Fortunately, the psychic shield we'd erected around our house turned it at the last minute.

This was the first house we'd ever bought, and it was well out in the Kentucky countryside. The closest "town" was around fifteen miles away, and had a population of around three thousand people. Even though we were far away from any major cities, I loved our new home. It gave me the time I'd always wanted to woods-walk and to study the local flora and fauna. I also had plenty of time to work on my writing.

The storm had passed, but the wind was still raging as my husband went to work and I began settling in for the night. I heard some banging outside and grabbed a flashlight to investigate. I assumed the trash cans had blown down and were smashing themselves against the house. All I wanted to do was get some sleep, not listen to Mother Nature play the drums all night.

Opening the door and shining the flashlight beam around, I saw nothing unusual; the garbage cans were secure against the house, not flying about the yard or crashing into the walls like I'd expected. I went down the steps and walked around the side of the house. Still nothing. I walked back around the house and began looking around our rather large backyard.

Suddenly I was overwhelmed by tremendous fear, bordering on panic. I moved the beam of light down the hill, sure that I would see a pack of rabid coyotes ready to spring on me.

There was only blackness between the cedar trees. No glowing eyes caught in the flashlight beam to indicate that any creature was skulking around in this tempest. But something had set off my psychic alarm. There was nothing unusual among the thick trees, but I sure wanted to get inside the house, and fast! I practically ran back into the safety of my home, quickly latching the storm and exterior doors as quietly as my panicked state would allow.

I slept fitfully that night, and dreamt of running away from a man with a gun who was trying to kill me. It was dark in the dream, but the terrain I was running through reminded me of the ravine behind our house, near a dirt road that was just off the main road a short distance from our driveway. That part of the ravine had always unsettled the kids and me, so we never spent much time there.

My husband came home early the next morning and I fixed him breakfast before he went to work at his day job. After that, I got Christopher, my son, on the bus for school.

Ever since we'd crossed Nimbi, my husband had begun to have a hard time with my spiritual work. He disliked any discussions of it. I had started taking Colette more into my confidence regarding the new psychic and occult side of my life. So that morning, I waited until she and I were alone in the house before bringing up the previous night's happenings.

"I was surprised I was afraid," I said as I sipped my cup of hot tea. "I don't fear the woods, but last night I was terrified."

Colette was now in high school, but was bored stiff because the classes were too easy for her. She had been in advanced classes in her last school, and this new district was at least two years behind the regular grade-levels of her old school, so we had decided to take her out and home-school her. Another burden at school was having to hide her "evil," as we jokingly called our pentacles, and she hated that. Our choice was either hide our Wiccan beliefs or wake up to a burning cross on the front lawn (in this highly prejudiced community, the KKK was firmly entrenched—if you weren't a white Christian male and/or growing pot, you were looked upon with suspicion).

"It sounds like we have a wayward down there," Colette said, in response to my story about the previous night. "You were probably just feeling the fear it experienced because of that tornado yesterday."

I wondered, sometimes, who was the adult here.

"God, I don't want to deal with another wayward," I said. "We just moved here and your daddy has been having a really hard time with all this stuff."

"We'll have to. I can help."

Not for the first time, I wondered whether this new job of crossing waywards was going to involve more than just our commitments. At the time I hoped not, but I also knew, in my heart of hearts, that neither Colette nor I would be able to refuse help to someone in need. This job seemed to be taking a turn toward becoming a career.

We put on our jackets and went for a walk, as we did every morning. The end of our road was a mile away from our house, and walking to the end and back gave us two miles worth of exercise. That was Colette's P.E. class. On the walk, we discussed how to find this wayward and how to convince it to go to the light. On the way back to the house, we took a short detour and went through the ravine off the dirt road. Colette could see the wayward hiding behind a stand of trees. She described her as a young woman, maybe eighteen or so. When she waved at her, the wayward waved back. This was a good start, since if the terror I'd felt the night before was the young woman's terror, it might take a little time before we could even try to cross her.

The next night was the full moon, so I thought it would be a great time to start. We could spend a little time in the ravine, convince the girl to go home, and we'd be done; right? Wrong! We spent an hour or so trying to convince her to go to the light, but all our efforts failed. The next day was a repeat of the day before. No success.

It would now be another month before the next full moon and our next chance to cross her (or so we thought, as beginners in the ghost-crossing business). So Colette did the only thing she thought might help—she invited the wayward back to our house. The young woman refused. Stubborn wayward. We kept asking her to come back with us, and within a few days she was our houseguest occasionally.

From our past experiences, Colette and I knew that you don't need to convince waywards they are dead in order to cross them; you just have to convince them to go to the light. Like most way-wards, this young woman thought she was alive and well. We felt that if she had any clue we considered her to be dead, she would lose her trust in us and never cross. So, during all our interactions with her, we had to keep up the ruse that she was physically alive. It became quite interesting.

Colette kept the young woman ghost company when she finally agreed to come back with us and spend a few hours at our house. But it felt like my daughter was having a friend over rather than trying to cross an earthbound soul. When my husband came home that evening, the wayward felt our tension about having her there and decided to leave.

Colette knew I had a Ouija board, even though we'd never used it. I kept it covered with a special tablecloth on my Wiccan altar at the end of my bed. I covered it to keep any negativity away from it, and my altar was blessed, so only positive vibrations would be associated with the game. But we got the Ouija board out soon after the wayward appeared, and tried to communicate with her. I was still quite unsure about a lot of things connected with cross-ing waywards, and felt I needed all the help I could get. We put the board on the coffee table between us and placed the pointer in the middle. Colette put her fingertips on the pointer.

"Come on, Mom, it won't bite." My daughter sounded much older than her fourteen years.

"I know," I said, perturbed at my own hesitation, and placed my fingertips lightly on the pointer as well. It began to move almost immediately.

"M-A-R-I-E" was spelled out on the lettered board. That was a good start; at least we had something to call her, now that it would be almost a month before we would again attempt to cross her. Marie then communicated, through the board, that the last thing she remembered was that she had been out on a date with her boyfriend, and he had taken her into the ravine to make out. He'd wanted to do more than she was comfortable with, and she'd run away from him. She heard a loud bang and fell down. That was the last thing she remembered; she had been running and hiding ever since.

It was obvious to us that Marie had been shot as she ran away from a potential rape. She did say she had seen a light, but she'd run away from it because she'd thought it was her boyfriend with a flashlight looking for her. It's amazing what a powerful force fear is—so powerful that it can keep us from going to the light when we die.

As we got to know Marie better, we started getting impressions from her (which is kind of like watching a movie playing in your head). She communicated a description of her boyfriend and the vehicle he was driving: the boyfriend was your basic redneck; the truck was a black, older-model Ford pickup. So, during those few weeks before the moon became full again, Colette and I went to the library a few times. Marie had given us a general date for when she went to the ravine: August 1982. We looked at the local papers, but found no reported deaths of a young woman by gunshot during that time. We began to think her body had never been found, and maybe her family thought she had run away. Or else she could have been from one of the many small towns in the area, and her disappearance just did not make the local paper. Or maybe we misinterpreted the date she'd given us.

We did, however, find an article about the local Rite Aid being robbed by two men in a black pickup truck around Christmastime in 1982; the truck matched the description Marie gave us of her boyfriend's truck. The man and his accomplice had been caught and jailed for two years for the crime. A physical description of the two men was not given in the article, but we were reasonably confident that one of them was the boyfriend. In another article, a few months after the Rite Aid robbery, a black pickup had been in a wreck, killing the driver and severely injuring the passenger. The driver had the same last name as the boyfriend. It had to have been connected; we didn't believe in coincidences.

At first, I'd had my doubts about this ghost. We'd found no real information about Marie's death, so I was beginning to think Colette and I were going crazy. But there were many signs that Marie was quite real. My puppy, Shiloh, would look at the couch beside me as we watched television and wag his tail. When I followed his line of sight, there was no one beside me. Also, when Marie began to spend the night with us (during the first week, she'd spent much of her time down in the ravine), she left evidence of her presence. The first morning after she stayed over, Colette dragged me into her room after her dad had left for work.

"Look," she said, pointing to the beanbag chair in the corner.

"Look at what?"

"There's an impression of a person in it," she said, excitement in her voice.

"That's where you've been sitting," I said, dismissing the subject and starting to walk toward her bedroom door.

"No," Colette insisted, "look at it. It looks like someone's been sleeping on it. Marie spent the night last night."

I turned around and looked closer, and was surprised. It did have a distinct silhouette of where someone had curled up in the fetal position. The depression where the head would have been was at one end. The rest of the body and the legs were going off the side of the giant pillow at the other end.

"Wow" was all I could say.

Over the next few weeks we had several other odd occurrences. For example, Marie bumped into the gate in the fence around our front yard and made it rattle. Our favorite thing that she did was change the channel on the television; she just didn't like what we were watching. My husband fussed about that for an hour afterwards! He just *knew* it was one of us who'd changed the channel suddenly, not the ghost who we said really did it. Another time, I left my cup of tea on the coffee table in front of the television while I gave Colette a homework assignment. When I went back to drink my tea, it was spilled. I asked Colette where the dogs were, and she said that they were under the table at her feet. After telling her that my tea had been spilled when no one was close to it, she said that Marie was standing behind her watching her do her lessons.

"Marie says she bumped into the table by accident, Mom. She says she's sorry."

"That's all right," I said, beginning to accept these strange happenings, and got a towel to clean up the mess. "How are you hearing her?"

"I don't know," Colette said thoughtfully. "At first I couldn't, and then I just tried really hard and I could."

"Do you have to speak out loud to her?"

"Yes. I haven't figured out how to talk to her with my thoughts yet. She does hear what you say as long as I'm around at the time."

"That's interesting," I said, putting the towel in the laundry. "How are you doing it?"

"I don't know … it's like … I hear what you say twice. Once for me, and once for her. It sounds like an echo in my head."

I decided I would try it. I turned on the television.

"Can Marie hear the television?"

"From me."

Concentrating, I tried to hear the echo. After a few minutes I did. "How about now?"

"She says it sounds like a stereo. She can hear it from both of us."

"Cool," I said. *Dead people hear me.*

Later that day, after trying several times, I was able to start communicating with Marie without Colette's help. But at first, while Colette could hear what our wayward was saying, I had to concentrate a little harder and could only get a feeling from Marie rather than actual words. Yet desire and determination can be powerful learning tools. Within a few days of steady trying, Colette had learned how to project her thoughts to Marie, as did I, so that neither of us had to speak out loud for her to hear us.

That fall, we had a few bad storms. One in particular awakened Colette, and she came into my room sometime after midnight.

"Mom, Marie's outside and she wants to come in."

"I thought she was staying in your room."

"Not all the time; she still goes back to the ravine. I think she feels uncomfortable around Dad."

"Sure, she can come in," I said as I got up.

"She says there's something creepy around our house."

"Is she talking about the shield?"

"I don't think so."

I tried to stay calm and wake up completely. I opened my psychic center to see what the problem was.

"The shield's up and looks like it always does," I said, still not too concerned.

Our shield is a psychic protection device. We imagine a bright white light starting in our solar plexus, and push it out around ourselves. We also push one out around a room, house, car...whatever...and it makes us feel safe by protecting us from dark forces. Colette had already told me that Marie could see our shield and could come through it. (We'd figured out by then that we could program the shield to split for "unawares," so that we, or anyone else, could come onto the property and through the shield without dissipating it or weakening it.)

"Yes, the shield's up," Colette replied. "But Marie says there's something crawling on it."

Trusting my daughter's abilities, I psychically looked at the shield a little more closely. I could in fact see dark things—the best way I can describe them—crawling all over it. They looked like distorted human shapes, with claws and talons instead of hands and feet. Their heads were grotesquely misshapen—some looked like bird heads (vultures), some looked like dinosaur heads. They were all very eerie.

"What are they?"

"I don't know," Colette said. I could tell she was frightened but trying not to show it.

I thought for a moment, the sleep clearing completely from my head. Somehow we needed to get Marie to come into the house so that she would be safe, just in case those creepy things decided to go after her.

"Tell Marie that we have special windows and doors, and she can come through them anytime she wants to come in and feel safe. The doors and windows will automatically open for her. Tell her that the creepy things are after us and won't hurt her. She'll be all right."

Up until this point we had always opened the door for Marie, allowing her to come in or go out. Since she still thought she was alive in a way, she wouldn't try to come through a closed door.

"Okay."

The concentration on my daughter's face was evident, even in the low light of the dark house. A few minutes later she relaxed.

"She's inside. It took me a while, but I finally convinced her to come in."

I breathed a sigh of relief, kissed Colette good night, and went back to bed myself. Before I went to sleep, I prayed for help in solving the creepy situation.

"I got an idea last night," I told Colette the next morning, after my son and husband had left for school and work.

"What was it?"

"The shield is like a computer, right?"

Colette nodded in agreement.

"It does what we tell it to."

"Yes."

"I think we can program it to catch those creepy things. Dark ones have such low vibrations that the ones on the other side cannot tune into them, but we can, since we are closer to their level of vibration. So I think we can snag the dark ones in the shield and then let the angels take them back to the other side, where they belong."

Over the next few days, I tried various ways of "catching" dark ones crawling on or near our shield. I found that I could make spikes in the shield and spear them, but I didn't necessarily want to harm any of them, just make them leave us alone. Next I tried throwing a net, made from the shield, over them. Some were able to move so quickly that the net missed, so I put that idea on hold.

I began thinking about the animal shows I loved to watch, the documentaries that showed lions and tigers (and bears, oh my!) in their natural habitats, fighting for survival. Camouflage and surprise, I concluded, would be the best way to go. I told the shield to reach out and grab any dark ones on it and hold them until the angels picked them up. Next I made the shield light up the area where the captured dark ones were, so the angels would be able to see them and take care of them.

You have to imagine that your shield is like a computer, with unlimited programming abilities and memory. There is only one thing, so far, that I've found the shield cannot do: two individual shields, once mixed together, cannot separate (only Mom and Dad can separate them). When Colette and I first put up our shields and allowed them to mix, our spirit guides informed us of this. However, when we were no longer in need of a particular shield (say, when I sold my Volvo and our shields were around it), the first person to go through the shields after we had relinquished ownership of the car would dissipate the them. We told the energy of the shields to go where it was needed at that point.

This incident, with Marie and the psychic shield, really got us thinking logically and deeply about our psychic techniques and procedures. In general, Marie taught us a lot about interacting with waywards. She may have been an inadvertent teacher, but we will always be very grateful for the lessons she gave. From the very first night, when I felt her fear in the ravine, she taught us how to speak to ghosts as well as how to pick up on what they are trying to communicate to us. She taught us to trust our instincts and believe that she was real—that we do exist after the death of our physical bodies.

After Marie had taught us these valuable lessons, the full moon drew near. Colette and I were both sad that she had to go, but we knew we couldn't keep her as a "pet." We had to figure out how to get her crossed without telling her she was dead. So we decided to have a party!

We invited several of Marie's favorite people who had already crossed. She liked *Gilligan's Island*, so we invited the Skipper and the Howells. She was a big fan of John Denver's, too, as well as Freddie Mercury (two of my personal favorites). I kept track of the odds of Marie crossing, based on our party list. At first it seemed like there was only a 50 percent chance of success, then 60 percent, then 75 percent. The party guest who convinced me we had a 100 percent chance of crossing Marie was Sybil Leek, a full-fledged witch that we knew Marie had begun to read about just before her death.

After all of these souls had graciously agreed to attend the party, we went down into the ravine with Colette's boom box. We played "Thank God I'm a Country Boy" and "You're My Best Friend." After we got through two songs, though, the boom box started messing up. Between the energy we were raising and the high vibrations from our guests from the other side, it was too much for the equipment, so we had to cut the party short. Eventually we all convinced Marie that the party would continue on the other side of the light, and she left with the celebrities.

It wasn't too bad. We'd fried the boom box, but it was worth it to have our pet wayward back where she needed to be ... where she now belonged ... home.

Afterword

With Marie, we had to use different tactics than we did with Nimbi. Nimbi just needed Jacob to encourage him to go, and a little push toward the light. Marie was still so fearful of her boyfriend that she remained stubborn about crossing until we offered too much temptation for her to resist. We'd spent so much time with her that we knew what would be most tempting to her.

It is worth noting that it took several days for Marie to become comfortable enough with us to begin to trust us, even a little. After we gained her trust, we could work on getting her more comfortable with the inevitable crossing, and the high spiritual vibrations that my children and I put out worked on getting her subconscious ready for her trip home as well.

Trust is a common theme with many of the waywards we deal with. I cannot stress enough that we don't lie to earthbound souls; this is one way to gain their trust. We just argue or discuss truths with them, until they logically understand that we are telling the truth and trust us. There is a lot of love involved in this type of work. If you don't have love in your heart, you will not be successful. As I've mentioned, there's a lot of desire and determination that goes into crossing a wayward, but love tempers everything we do. Even with the stubborn and cranky waywards.

As Colette and I went into the ravine to cross Marie, we began to raise our vibrations in the hopes that Marie would cross as soon as the spirits from the other side came to the party; of course, we prayed and meditated as well. After getting to the spot in the ravine where Marie had died, our energy escalated even more with the presence of the ones from the other side. That was the first and only time, so far, that we have asked for that much "firepower" from the other side. It could happen again, but for the most part, the crossing process just involves us preparing the soul, and the soul realizing that he or she does not belong on the earthly plane anymore. Marie's party was what we call divine intervention—where Mom and Dad help in some way other than just moral support.

There is divine intervention in other stories in this book as well, but it occurs in different ways. In general, divine intervention can take many forms—from something as small as getting a late start preventing you from being in an accident (this has happened to me twice so far), to something larger. One time, for example, there was an ice storm that caused my divorce hearing to be postponed a month. I only received notification of the original hearing two days after the date—the day after the ice melted. I hadn't known to go to the courthouse on the specified date, and for some reason that I'm still unaware of, Mom and Dad felt the hearing needed to be held at a later date.

When conducting crossings, Colette and I want the ghosts to *want* to cross over; that way, they are the ones who cause the tunnel of light to open. We can open the tunnel ourselves, as you'll see in a later story, but that takes a lot of energy, so we try to get the wayward to think about the light. This allows us to use our energy for the push the ghost needs to eventually cross over.

Because of the expenditure of energy involved in crossings, regardless of who opens the tunnel of light, we always ground afterwards: we eat, or do some type of physical exercise like take a walk or clean the house. Even going over mathematical equations can ground you. This helps to keep the spirit, housed in the physical body, balanced. If you keep your vibrations at a high level all the time, you will have problems going about your physical life. All of us still have to work and keep a household running, and we have to take care of our physical selves to accomplish these tasks. Existence in the physical realm is mainly about learning how to love under difficult conditions, but it is all about learning. Learning to have balance in your life is part of living in the physical world.

Walmart Waywards

"Mom," my son Christopher said as we walked to the restroom at the front of the Walmart, "there's a boy next to me and he has his head all bandaged up."

I looked down at my youngest child; he was twelve years old. The next words he said really shocked me.

"I can see through him," he whispered.

"Did he say anything to you?" I asked, as goose bumps flooded my skin. I knew my son was talking about a wayward.

Looking at the space beside my son, I could see the boy in my mind's eye. He was taller than Christopher, probably around fourteen or fifteen years old, and dressed in what looked like loose pajamas. It finally dawned on me why I had been nursing a headache

55

within ten minutes of entering the store. There was something negative about this place; my headache was my higher self, warning me about the negativity. Right now I just couldn't deal with the ghost standing next to us.

"No, he didn't say anything, he just tugged at my shirt like this," Christopher said, and demonstrated by tugging three times on my blouse.

"Okay, baby, don't worry about him. We'll help him later."

"Somebody hurt him," Christopher insisted.

"I know, baby. Nobody will hurt him again. We'll show him home and he'll feel a lot better after that."

"He's still standing here."

Again, goose bumps flooded my skin and "a little creeped out" just doesn't begin to describe my feelings at that moment.

"Go use the bathroom with your daddy, but don't say anything to him about the boy," I said, trying to remind Christopher of his original reason for coming to the front of the store.

In the women's room, I told Colette about the wayward her brother had seen.

"There's a lot more than just that one kid, Mom," she said as we washed our hands. "I saw a bunch when we were in the back of the store."

"Why didn't you tell me sooner?"

"Because of Daddy," she said, in that older-than-fifteen voice of hers. "That kind of stuff freaks him out and I don't want him getting pissed off in Walmart. He's just going to start bitching about how we're all crazy. Just because he can't see—"

"All right, I get the point," I said, deciding to stop her rant before it got to be a full-blown bitch session about her dad. "He really does love you, baby, he just doesn't see this stuff like we do. We're going to have to figure out what to do about these waywards." I rubbed my forehead.

"Fine."

"Do you have a headache?" I asked suddenly.

"Yeah, I do."

"I think it's just the negativity here. We'll get out of here as soon as we can."

I looked back at the Walmart as we drove away, and could almost see the darkness surrounding the building.

Over the next few days, Colette and I discussed the Walmart waywards. There had once been a state hospital for the mentally ill a few blocks behind this Walmart, and we did some research on the Internet about it. Originally, the hospital grounds had extended to where the back of the Walmart building now was located. I could only imagine what kind of horrors the people confined there had gone through in the early half of the twentieth century: lobotomies, shock treatments, and abuse from each other as well as from the staff.

After we were satisfied with the research results, we began devising a game plan. We figured there were a lot of waywards there, but getting them all crossed over would be a challenge. A challenge Colette and I were going to take on—and complete—no matter how long it took. We also realized that trying to use the full moon's power would not always be an option with this massive crossing. Trying to time our trips to Walmart, eighty miles away, by the lunar cycles—without telling my husband why—would be ... well ... lunacy.

Colette and I prayed for help on how to begin this massive cross-over of waywards. We received impressions about three of the almost 170 ghosts that were connected to the state hospital. These three had been committed because they heard voices no one else could hear, or they saw things no one else could see. They were not mentally ill, just misunderstood. They had been psychic enough to hear their spirit guides or other people's thoughts, or maybe even see ghosts, but they certainly were not crazy. Before people began to be more accepting of psychic phenomena, those who experienced it and told someone about their abilities ended up, most of the time, in an insane asylum or accused of being in league with Satan.

These three waywards would be the key, we decided. We should be able to cross them easily, and hoped they would come back to help us with the others—at the very least, the others would follow them into the light. Everyone has free-will choice, regardless of whether they are physical or not, and it would be this free-will choice that we would be tapping into and relying on to get everyone crossed.

Our next trip to Walmart didn't occur until several months later, and Colette and I took full advantage of it. After we entered the store, we told my husband that we needed some personal supplies, which we knew would keep him away from us (he avoided "female" shopping at all costs). He and Christopher went off in another direction as Colette and I headed toward the women's aisle. We were careful to stay away from the checkouts and any other computer-operated devices. We'd learned, from crossing Marie, that the massive amount of energy we would be dealing with would wreak havoc on the equipment, and we wanted to conduct this cross-over quickly and quietly. We hoped, also, that no one would find out, especially my husband.

"You need to go to the light," I whispered softly as soon as we felt two of our target waywards around us. The third one came quickly as the tunnel of light opened.

The first two waywards hightailed it to the light, and the third was hot on their heels. The tunnel opening so fast drew the attention of several other waywards. Unfortunately, the others had just gathered to see what the commotion was about; they weren't going through the tunnel.

"There's a party on the other side of that light," I began, not really sure of where I was going with this thought at first. "There is cake and ice cream, cookies and milk. Your friends are already enjoying themselves."

Was there really a party on the other side? I had confidence there was. We were doing God's work and God could provide anything. We were again thankful to Marie for what she had inadvertently taught us about what we could do, and about what the ones on the other side could do.

About then, the three "normal" waywards came back through the tunnel and verified what we were saying. I still couldn't hear what they were saying, for the most part, but I did understand the emotions. The emotions almost always outweigh the words; sometimes the words and emotions are the same. At the same time, I could feel disbelief from the uncrossed waywards. Suddenly an idea came to me.

"There are no doctors or nurses at the party," I said softly, "and if you need to find out if someone is there, there are people there who can help. They'll tell you who is at the party and who is not there." I figured that this would prevent problems if any of the waywards started asking us about specific people.

After I said this, the trickle of earthbound souls going through the tunnel became a flood. Then it went back to a trickle; then nothing. The tunnel closed, and we had crossed less than a third of them. It was a good accomplishment for our first try at such a massive undertaking; unfortunately, there were still over a hundred waywards left. I was somewhat disappointed, but still sure that we could get them all. It would just take time. My desire and determination to cross waywards was growing; I figured it would eventually come close to the obsession level (obsession may not be a strong enough word, though). This was definitely turning into a career.

Colette and I looked around after the tunnel closed. No lights had gone off, or even flickered. None of the electrical equipment had gone haywire, and when we passed the registers, they all seemed to be functioning properly.

Within two minutes of the tunnel closing, my husband and son came around the corner of the aisle, and we left with our camouflage of personal items. It would be almost a year before we could make it back to that Walmart.

The next time we were there, we used the same tactic we'd used during the first crossing: my husband and Christopher went shopping, and Colette and I headed for the feminine aisle. This time, as well as mentioning the cake and ice cream, we said that the party was a costume party; there were costumes available on the other side of the light. And we had a little help with this crossing, as well. Physical people who could astral project came to help us (in astral projection, the spirit form leaves the physical form and is able to travel freely). This helped tremendously; the astral body is closer to the vibrations of the waywards, just a small step down from wayward frequency, so they were able to see and even touch the waywards. One of our astral friends, a big guy we call William, got tired of the waywards standing around and not going to the light, so he began pushing them into the tunnel! We could only giggle at his impatience.

The only potential problem with this was keeping the astrals from going to the light too. Home is where we all belong and even in the physical realm, some of us can still feel homesick when we're near a tunnel of light (like when we're at a relative's deathbed when they die). An astral has to have tremendous willpower not to go to the light. If an astral did go to the light, his or her physical body would lapse into a coma, because there would be no spirit to animate it. I had grown used to having my astral friends around and did not want this to happen to them, so Colette and I stayed between them and the light as much as possible.

At one point during all this, we saw a physical woman and her daughter come down the aisle where we had opened the tunnel. Colette and I both visibly tensed. We were afraid they would frighten away the gathering ghosts. Suddenly, the girl seemed to notice us and turned to her mother.

"No," she said, "what I need is in the other aisle."

They left with no harm done. The wayward exodus continued uninterrupted. Did the girl see the tunnel and the waywards, or did she just sense something supernatural going on? Did it frighten her? Whatever the case, they left, and we continued our work. That was a close one.

Half of those who were left went to the light that day. We felt confident that we would get the rest crossed over on our next try.

During this period of time, my personal problems with my husband were intensifying. He hated that I was becoming more psychic, and felt that I was keeping things from him. I was in fact keeping the wayward wrangling from him, since it seemed to upset him that I could see and communicate with individuals when he could not.

Soon after my husband and I separated, Colette and I made our last trip to Walmart. Before this trip, I'd dreamed that I was to think of a shield—a kind of net—and put it around the area, gathering as many waywards in it as I could. So, when Colette and I walked to the back of the store and stopped in front of a display of movies, I began concentrating on the wayward net. I imagined it flowing up and out of my solar plexus and encompassing the entire building. I pictured it looking like an umbrella that dropped down to the ground, but with a high dome that reached to the top of the building. Then slowly, I began to close the net, as if catching fish. The ones on the other side opened the tunnel with our help. We just had to concentrate on the tunnel of light, and it slowly appeared.

At about the point when I'd pulled the net halfway through the building, I noticed a young man in a Walmart vest staring at me. I wondered what he saw, if anything. My concentration couldn't falter, so I ignored him and continued my task. I wasn't about to lose any waywards because I couldn't do my job.

We got all but one earthbound soul into our ghost net and gently forced them through the tunnel of light. The last one took a few minutes to talk over. And that was the end of the Walmart waywards.

Afterword

This was the first, and so far the only, crossing of this magnitude that Colette and I have ever attempted. There are rarely this many waywards in one place. We usually meet one or two, but hardly any more than that at one time. Usually, you need to spend some quality one-on-one time with a ghost in order to gain his trust and cross him to the other side. With these waywards, however, we had time constraints to deal with.

Why were all these ghosts earthbound? I really feel that they had lost their hope of there being a better place than where they died. Being mentally impaired doesn't always mean that a soul will go wayward, but in some cases, it does. We have also found that when one or more in this type of group stays earthbound, more follow; one wayward can start a cascade effect. The waywards become lost and just don't know where to go. The lights that were in their institution probably didn't help, either, because when the tunnel of light opened for them to cross, they felt fear, or were confused about crossing.

With the Walmart waywards, I can't say that Colette and I really prepared for the crossing through any kind of visualization or breathing exercises. It would have been impossible, given the circumstances. We were just so determined to cross them that nothing else seemed to matter. Desire and determination, as I have said before, are powerful influences. Tempered with love, they can work miracles.

Why did the idea of a party on the other side come to me? I still haven't figured that one out, but as long as it worked, all were happy. These poor souls had been so mistreated for so long and were in such depths of depression that I guess a party sound quite good to them. They needed the hope that this escape provided for them, and they were willing to take a chance and trust us. As long as it works and you don't lie to a wayward, that's all that matters.

By our last trip to Walmart, Colette and I were really getting into the swing of crossing waywards. Not only had we learned things from Marie, but we'd done several other crossings as well, quick ones where we just had to tell the wayward to go to the light. (The stories of some of these souls, like the hitchhiker and the man who didn't like pigeons, are included in the chapters that present multiple waywards.)

The issue of people observing you while you're crossing a wayward is an interesting one. With the Walmart ghosts, two physical individuals noticed that something was out of the ordinary. These people must have seen or felt something about us doing this type of work. Other than these two people, nobody else in the store noticed anything unusual around them. Some people who are close to the work that Colette and I do experience strange things (as the next story will show). Dwayne, my fiancé, has seen and felt things associated with a few of the earthbound souls that we have dealt with, but then again, he lives with us and is psychically sensitive to begin with.

Colette and I have not crossed every wayward we've become aware of, but we have crossed every one we've tried to. It may seem a bit odd that we have a perfect success rate, but, in short, we don't give the ghosts a choice. Regarding concerns about free-will choice and what earthbound souls want, well...we treat waywards as childlike individuals. Every child wants to grow up. This is a subconscious desire. A child may want to play with a shiny knife, but you would be ten times a fool to allow that to happen. You wouldn't give a child the free-will choice to play in the middle of a busy interstate or the free-will choice to play with fire. It is not in children's best interest to allow them to endanger themselves. It's pure stupidity. I go by one principle when crossing waywards: every wayward wants to go home. No matter what the circumstances surrounding their deaths, home is where they need to go when the physical body dies. A ghost may desire to continue with his routine, or get revenge, or pursue any number of other goals, but that is not in its best interests; going home is.

Colette and I have talked about this at length. She feels that after one of her lives, she went wayward and received help from a physical person to cross over. She says that the feeling is very much like being locked in a room and unable to open the door to get out, if you even know that the door exists. It's like being in self-imposed solitary confinement. You can't move on until you get help—occasionally it's divine help, but most of the time it's from someone in the physical world. If you think about ghosts in this way, you'll understand what I'm saying. When you need help, you ask for it; but a wayward can't always be heard when it asks for help. This can be frustrating for the ghost.

The Men in Gray

"The Gates of Hell Cemetery?" I asked as my daughter and her two friends got out of the van. We were parked in the grass at the end of the dirt road. "What a banal nickname."

We walked under the rusted archway into the 175-year-old graveyard.

Colette and I had come to the cemetery at the urging of her friends Dan and Dawn. They had heard of some local "witches" and teenagers trying to contact the dead, and they wanted us to see what we could do about the eerie feelings people reported experiencing in the area. Both had also heard of people coming to the graveyard at Halloween and full moons and doing all kinds of weird things, like sacrificing animals and such. The past several years, though, neighbors had been calling the local police whenever they saw a vehicle go too far down this dead-end road, especially at night. I hoped that coming here when it was still light out would increase our chances of not having to deal with the police.

I knew that Jane (the woman whose son Jacob had called Nimbi to him) had been right when she'd told me we were protected as long as we were doing God's work. At the same time, I wasn't going to be stupid about our safety; I wanted to get this investigation over with as soon as possible. I was hoping we could spend a few minutes figuring out what we had to do, get our work done, and leave. I was in the process of going through my divorce at this time; it was still not finalized, and I didn't want to give my soon-to-be-ex-husband any more fuel to use against me. He'd already accused me of being "a Satan-worshiping witch," in court and to anyone who would listen to him in our highly Christian community. Colette and I had already moved to a new home, not only to find work but for safety's sake (skinheads were making threats against our lives).

We weren't really expecting to find too much at the cemetery, even though people playing around with psychic stuff in graveyards, thinking it's all a bunch of mumbo jumbo, can get stuff started that they can't control once it's given life. Not surprisingly, they rarely consider safety factors and the containment of these energies.

"The Gates of Hell," I repeated mockingly. "No wonder every teenager in the area has to come here to make out or try to call up some demon. Good God."

"It's called that because the people who are buried here were never baptized. They were 'unsaved,'" Dan explained. "And therefore going to hell."

"Well, I know hell doesn't want me, and heaven isn't ready for me yet," I said with a cynical laugh.

"Only a bunch of Christian elitists could name a cemetery for unbaptized people 'The Gates of Hell,'" Colette said, her laugh echoing mine.

"Christians are the ruling majority in this country. I'm sure that everyone buried here didn't go to hell." I tried to temper my daughter's anger before it got out of hand. "We came here for a reason," I reminded her. "To fix the problems that were caused by dabblers and upstarts, not to mention the drunk fools with battered copies of the *Necronomicon*."

"You're right. Sorry."

We were fairly deep into the graveyard by now. "I feel something near that tree," I said. I looked around and saw a swirl of whitish gray clouds moving slowly counterclockwise, centered on the oldest and biggest tree in the cemetery.

"Yeah," Colette said. "It looks like some idiots tried to open a psychic portal."

"Think we can close it up?"

"Piece of cake."

"Chocolate, of course," I said, and laughed. The four of us formed a circle around the huge old oak tree.

Dawn looked at Dan, and Dan looked at me. "So...what do we do now?" he asked.

"Just give us your energy and we'll do the rest," I said. I closed my eyes, trying to block out all other distractions. "Just think positive and loving thoughts."

After a while we were able to reverse the portal and seal it, but it drained me. I really should have begged out of this whole trip, but I felt that I had to be there to help...in any way I could. Plus, with an adult around, it would be easier for the police to believe we were just looking around and not sacrificing something. (I was still hoping they wouldn't show up.)

Exhaustion overcame me, and I sat down on the cool early evening grass to rest for a minute. I was glad we'd decided to visit the cemetery before dark for several reasons. Not only would the police would be less likely to be called on us, but it was easier to see what we were doing, physically speaking, when it was light out, as opposed to feeling our way around in the dark with flashlights (and the flashlights themselves would have attracted unwanted attention.)

"I'm feeling a dark one in the woods. He's watching us," my daughter whispered to me. "He's got a real problem with Dawn. I think he might have been a slave owner or a slave runner when he was physical. He seems to be looking for an escapee."

Dawn's mother was German and her father was black. My thought was that she might draw the dark presence close enough for Colette to "grab" it and send it home. We had "grabbed" dark ones before, with our house shield, and pushed them up for the angels to take back home, but we had never done it before with our personal shields. It shouldn't be much different, should it?

"See if Dawn wants to help; explain to her what you're thinking, and take Dan with y'all."

Colette told them what was going on and asked if they were up to it. Both of them agreed enthusiastically.

I sat there watching carefully as they pushed through the undergrowth. I knew I should have brought something to eat, so I could have grounded myself after raising and directing so much energy while closing that half-assed portal. I would definitely remember a snack for everyone involved the next time.

Suddenly there was a loud crack. I jumped up at the sound and saw Colette pulling hard on Dawn's arm. Dan jumped back at that same moment, and just as he got clear, a large branch slammed to the ground in the spot where they had been standing.

"Are you okay?!" I shouted.

"Just barely," Colette shouted back. Dawn and Dan were shouting nervously about what had happened.

I knew by the tone of Colette's voice that she was more determined than ever to get the dark one. Once that child gets something in her mind, she dogs it until she gets something accomplished. She's like a beagle or a pit bull. She can argue a stop sign into turning into a green "go" sign. That's what makes her such a good ghost hunter.

I sat back down, then lay down on the grass and listened as Colette bulled her way back into the woods. I tried to ground myself. I imagined roots growing from my body, going down into the damp earth.

"What are you doing here?" I felt a commanding voice say, a few minutes later.

I didn't open my eyes; I knew a wayward had found me. I was becoming used to being a "ghost magnet," and it hardly fazed me anymore.

"I'm grounding," I told him matter-of-factly.

Opening my psychic eyes, I saw that he was a Confederate soldier. I secretly hoped that he was the only ghost around.

"You shouldn't be here."

"I know. I just had to rest for a bit," I said, trying to project my southern drawl, hoping it would calm his anxiety at finding me being there.

"You need to leave. It's dangerous here."

He seemed genuinely interested in protecting me from whatever danger he perceived was present at the time he had died. I was truly impressed with his gallant emotions.

"I know," I said, not moving from my prone position.

Calling my spirit guide, I gleaned as much information as he was able to give me about this proud gentleman before I began the work of helping him home. I asked several times for clarification, but all I got was a sense of longing and uncertainty. I had to figure things out for myself, as usual. Suddenly I got a flash from "Axe

Man of Miner's Creek," one of the stories in *Phantoms Afoot* by Mary Summer Rain. I had already learned to trust these kind of insights, and plunged full throttle into my fast-developing plan.

Turning my attention back to the wayward, I began.

"I've actually been looking for you. There's someone who would like to see you again."

There was disbelief coming from the man who squatted near my feet. I could see his gray uniform; the thick, heavy wool jacket was unbuttoned, exposing a loosely woven white shirt, and he seemed somewhat thin for his big-boned frame. He cradled his rifle loosely in his arms, resting it on his knees as he did so. He continued to squat at my feet.

"I wouldn't know who that could be," he said, pulling back slightly.

I had a brief thought that I was losing him, but I pressed on gently.

"It's someone you love very much, and who loves you back the same way," I said, not really sure who it was, just following the feelings I was getting from my spirit guide. I tried hard to pull the information forward. There was someone on the other side … who was it? A female. A sister? His mother? There, I had it. The tunnel of light was beginning to form.

"She misses you and wants you to be with her. She's waiting for you in that light."

He looked above and over me. I could feel his resistance and disbelief, but I pushed on.

"Go to her, she's waiting."

"I don't know who you're talking about."

"She's in the light. Do you see her?"

"No."

Damn stubborn Southerner ghost.

"Look closer."

"I don't see … " There was a pause. "Mary? MARY!"

I felt him jump up and run to the light. I breathed a sigh of relief. In my head, Freddie Mercury was singing, "Another one bites the dust." I smiled broadly.

After grounding for a while longer, I got up and began to wander around the graveyard. Cemeteries have always been such peaceful places for me. I've liked visiting them ever since I was a child. This was only the third graveyard I'd found with a ghost in it. I know ... most people seem to think ghosts gravitate to cemeteries, but they don't. They're usually found in the area where their physical body died or where they have some kind of emotional connection, such as their home or a loved one's home. Sometimes they even attach themselves to an inanimate object, like a piece of furniture or a personal possession.

As I walked back toward the rusted archway, I felt strange. Someone was watching me. Looking around, I saw no one physical.

"Hello?" I said, again projecting thoughts of love and compassion.

"Are you supposed to be here?"

Another wayward, I thought to myself. *What the hell is going on with this place? Could the dabblers have somehow pulled waywards to this dilapidated cemetery?*

"Sorry, I'm a little lost. I'm looking for my home," I replied quite naturally. "They left a light on for me. Could you help me find it?"

"There's no houses 'round here."

It was another Confederate soldier. Obviously, these guys were still fighting the Civil War. While the first one had been somewhat clean-shaven, this one had a big handlebar moustache. And he was right ... there were no houses around here; just corn fields and cow pastures.

"I'm sure it's around somewhere. They left the light on for me. It's a really bright light ... the light of home."

I could feel the soldier look around.

"I see it. It's not too far."

The portal was opening. That now-familiar queasiness was building in my solar plexus.

"Would you like to come with me? My family will welcome you. You could get some rest."

"I really need to stay with the rest of the men. We're waiting for further orders from our captain."

Great. There were more waywards here, but at least now I had a clue as to how to cross the others when I found them. I was a little surprised I didn't feel them already, but first things first.

"Just come over for a little bit," I said.

I wasn't going to give him a chance to go back to his friends. He needed to cross over. I'd deal with the others soon enough.

As I walked toward that beautiful tunnel, I felt him follow me. A happy, homesick feeling washed over me as I walked through the light. He crossed. I stayed. One day it would be my turn.

As I continued walking, looking for the rest of the soldiers, a brilliant purple light hit me with enough force that it nearly knocked me back a step. My solar plexus was now feeling sore from all the psychic energy I was expending. I figured the purple light was from the energy of a wayward in the ravine I was approaching. I looked down the hill, but could see nothing, only feel a strong anger. Whoever it was did not want me to see him. It felt like someone had a lot of righteous anger about something; maybe being murdered?

Great. There was a lot more work to do. But right now I felt I needed to find the Confederate soldiers who were still wandering around without physical bodies.

About then Colette and her friends returned. She'd been successful and hadn't had too many more problems. She began to talk about it fervently. I wanted to know everything, but had to stop her from telling me right then because I needed her help finding the rest of the waywards. She had a lot more energy than I did. I thought about sending her after the more difficult ghost down the hill while I concentrated on the Confederates. The first two had been easy; whoever was left shouldn't be that difficult, but they might be suspicious of us because of Dawn's dark skin. So I told Colette about the wayward in the small gorge and sent her on her way; Dawn and Dan went with her.

I stood at the top of the hill and sensed the men. They were camped out about halfway down the hill. The camp was on a pretty good incline, so I had to make my way carefully. I didn't get far before I was challenged again.

"What are you doing here?"

"I'm just a little lost, but I think I'm looking for y'all," I said, trying to appear nonthreatening while concentrating on speaking like I would have in the 1860s. "I'm a little hard of hearing and can't see very well; you'll have to forgive me."

"That's all right, ma'am," a dark-haired young man said as he came up beside me, taking my elbow so he could guide me to their camp. "My name is Shawnee."

"We'll help you down the hill," another man said as he took my other elbow.

There was a strong sense of chivalry among these men. It quite surprised me; it made me almost giddy.

"Thank you, gentlemen," I said as I allowed their help; I was sure they hadn't helped someone in a very long time and it was like they relished the idea of helping a damsel in distress. I stopped where the main part of their camp was. Everyone was standing, out of politeness for me.

"I was sent here by your general. He wants y'all to go to that light. He said he'll have more orders for y'all on the other side of the light."

An older man, probably the one in command, started giving orders to pack up and get moving. I watched as all ten of them filed through the light and were gone. There had been an even dozen Confederate soldiers all together.

I climbed back up the hill and met Colette, Dawn, and Dan under the archway of the cemetery.

"Did you get that other guy, down in the ravine?"

"Yeah, he wanted to kill the man who murdered him. I argued him to the other side," Colette said.

"I knew you would, baby!"

"Can we go home now?" the three of them asked. "We're hungry."

"I'm ready," I told them, fishing my keys out of my pocket.

"I want pizza."

"Yeah, and how about that chocolate cake you mentioned earlier?"

"We'll see," I said, as the light began to fade at the Gates of Hell.

Afterword

You are probably wondering how exactly my daughter managed to cross the dark wayward in the woods. The ghost was in fact a slave owner looking for a runaway, and even though Dawn knew it would be dangerous, she agreed to be the "bait." Eventually, Dawn standing out in the open proved to be too much of a temptation for the dark wayward. Colette hid behind a tree, and when the wayward got close enough to Dawn, Colette was able to grab him by projecting her personal shield around him. Then she pushed him up so the angels could take him home.

We went to the Gates of Hell Cemetery for one reason, but found several other reasons for our presence there—and they were all wayward. This was definitely a case in which Colette's and my inner spirits were led somewhere we had a job to do—even if we weren't consciously aware of it to begin with.

Our friends on the other side try to give us enough information so that we can be ready if we encounter a wayward who has lost his way. Most of the time, though, I feel like I'm flying by the seat of my pants, not to mention stumbling along in this unique job of mine. This whole ghost-hunting thing has been a trial by fire from the very start. We have to think on our feet most of the time and improvise—a lot. But it's worth it to help lost souls back home.

When doing this work, it's important to remember that God protects you; nevertheless, you don't want to abuse this protection. We were highly aware that we were in a graveyard where the police were often called to run off or arrest trespassers. It's like that old joke about the guy in the flood:

> Rain had come down for days and flood waters were approaching a man's house. A man in a four-wheel drive came up and asked the man if he wanted to go to higher ground.
>
> "No," the man replied. "God's going to save me."
>
> The floodwaters came up to the man's porch, and a man in a boat came to him and asked if he wanted to move to higher ground.
>
> "No," the man replied. "God's going to save me."
>
> The flood then forced the man to climb onto his roof, where a helicopter came by to rescue him.
>
> "No," the man said. "God's going to save me."
>
> The man drowned and went to heaven.
>
> "Why didn't you save me, God?" he asked.
>
> "What do you mean?" God told him. "I sent you a truck, a boat, and a helicopter!"

So, no, we don't disregard the world around us just because we have faith in God's protection. Sometimes, physical hints are in fact from God. If someone had come by and told us the police had been called, we would have high-tailed it out of there, not waited for God's hand to pick us up and move us away from the "danger." Moral of the story: if you're in a flood and a guy in a truck comes by to get you to higher ground, don't spit in God's face—take the ride you're offered!

This was also one of very few times when we encountered a wayward who was dangerous in a physical sense. The dark ghost was able to manipulate the energy around him—he caused a branch to fall down. If it had not been for Colette's quick reactions, one or more of the group could have been seriously injured. But this is a fact of wayward wrangling. We have learned to constantly be on our toes when we go into any spiritual investigation. We never know what we will find. Flying by the seat of your pants isn't always dangerous, but it can be. Quick thinking can keep you safe in many situations, but this is a job where you need to be at the top of your form. For example, we don't go to places where there could be an earthbound soul if we are intoxicated in any way. It's not that we don't have an occasional glass of wine; we just don't do it when we suspect there could be waywards around.

I think that the act of lying down to ground myself was what helped me feel the other ghosts around me. I had been unaware of them up until then. Also, I had extremely low spiritual energy at that time, having just gotten away from a psychic vampire (energy vacuums as I call them) in my own life; I was unable to tune in to the waywards' higher vibrations until I'd replenished myself by grounding with Mom Earth's energy, which she gladly shares with us.

The techniques I used in several of the crossings that day were inspired by my reading. With the first wayward, as mentioned, I remembered a story where a ghost crossed after seeing his woman in the tunnel of light. The crossing of the whole platoon was inspired by the story "Madness in Bogan Flats," from the same book. Mary Summer Rain and her husband convinced a wayward that a wagon master wanted to hire him to scout a new territory. I, in turn, told the Confederate soldiers that they needed to go to the light to get their new orders.

If you choose to and are able to do this work, take ideas and nudges from this book or others ... or television shows, movies, songs ... and apply them to crossing waywards. Listen to your inner promptings. If you get a flash of insight from one or more of these stories or songs, take advantage of it. This is how the other side communicates with us. As a society, we have never had so many outlets as we have now when it comes to entertainment, and this can provide many symbols and references for communicating with the other side. Interpreting your dreams is a tremendous help as well.

There's always the question of why these earthbound souls didn't cross at the time of their deaths. Well, the dark one knew, on some level, that the place he would go was not a good one. Hell is not fire and brimstone; it's your worst fears realized. If you are deathly afraid of snakes, then they will crawl all over you, chase you, bite you, whatever, the whole time you're there. What is worse? Well, the fact that you have also separated yourself from God. To us, that is far worse than having snakes or spiders crawling all over you. Hell is also a place where you have to relive the areas where you went wrong in your chart, over and over again, until you learn not to make those bad choices.

From Colette, I learned that the wayward in the ravine did indeed want revenge for his murder. These waywards can also be very difficult to cross, especially if they know they're dead (which about half the time they do). But they can be crossed. Once a soul has crossed, it knows that everything will be fine in the physical world it left behind: people, things, and attitudes. Once the man bent on revenge crossed, he realized that the one who murdered him would have to pay for that grievous act; if not in this lifetime, then in another. Not to mention the fact that he would have to relive the murder until he learned not to take a life. We all eventually have to accept responsibility for what we do.

The reason the Confederate soldiers didn't cross at death was because they had a sense of duty that kept them earthbound. The first two felt a longing for loved ones or their family that eventually overpowered this skewed sense of duty. The rest of the platoon was just waiting for their next assignment, so it was rather easy to cross them. And we did not lie to any of these waywards.

Quick Waywards

As I've mentioned before, some waywards take almost no effort to cross. This chapter presents stories of these "quick" waywards.

Injun Joe

My friend Fran stopped me at the coffee machine where we work. "I have a photo I want you to look at, and tell me—"

"The answer is yes," I said.

"Let me get out the question first!" Fran said, laughing.

I shrugged as I laughed, too. "I just know that the answer to your question is yes."

Fran gave me a teasing, exasperated look. "It looks like there's some sort of spirit in this photo," she said, pulling out her digital camera and pushing buttons until she found the picture. It was a photo of her Toyota MR2 (a very small, two-door car). It had a tiny trailer hooked onto the back of it. There was a large, wispy swirl of colors at the end of the trailer, covering the lower half of the picture. A face could be seen in this kaleidoscope of foggy colors.

"Was there any fog the evening you took this picture?" I asked, knowing that Fran and her husband lived near a lake.

"No, it was clear, and neither of us saw anything near the trailer until we looked at the picture. Neither of us was smoking, either."

"You've got yourselves a wayward."

"A what?"

"A ghost—an earthbound soul."

I closed my eyes to block out some of the distractions in our workplace, a home improvement warehouse.

"He's a Native American who lived by himself. His white name was Injun Joe. He wore a denim vest with blue jeans and a flannel shirt, and moccasins he made himself."

"How do you know this?" Fran asked.

"I don't know. I was just seeing this guy in my mind's eye."

"What can I do?"

"Do you want to learn how to cross waywards?" I asked, grinning mischievously. I knew that Fran and her husband, George, had been getting in touch with their Native American spiritual roots over the last several months, and I wanted to see if I could teach her how to cross waywards.

"Uh…" was her response.

"It might be easy. But if you and George can't cross him, I'll come out."

"Why is he hanging around us?"

"You live where he used to. He likes to watch y'all work. You've probably felt him around you occasionally."

"Well, yeah," she said slowly. I could tell that she was thinking about it. "That kind of 'someone's watching over my shoulder' feeling?"

"Yes. Now all you have to do is light a candle or start a fire," I said. My fiancé Dwayne and I had been out to Fran and George's house, and I knew they had just built a nice fire pit in their backyard. It would be perfect. "Waywards are attracted to natural light. They can't see incandescent or fluorescent lights. Then y'all just need to talk about the light and how beautiful it is on the other side. Then tell him to go to the light."

"All right," she said, but I could tell she was unsure.

"It'll be easy. I really think he's just confused. He should go quickly."

We both went back to work.

The next day we were working together again.

"Hey, Anson, I wanted to talk to you some more about our ghost."

"He crossed," I said, as soon as the impression came to me.

"But we didn't do anything."

"Did y'all discuss the wayward last night?"

"Yes, but just what you had said to me. We didn't light a candle or anything."

"That's all right. Did you say anything about the light?"

"Sure."

"That's all it took. Sometimes they're that easy." I giggled at Fran's astonishment. "See how easy it can be? How do you like being a Ghost Buster?"

"It's weird."

Mentioning the Light

There have been other instances where all it took was mentioning the light. Once, we saw a earthbound soul hitchhiking, carrying a gas can while walking along the interstate. All we had to do was pull over and offer him a ride to the nearest gas station; then we told him that the gas station on the other side of the light had better gas than the one we dropped him off at, and he was gone.

Then there was a man in a field, who was just wandering around until Colette told him to look for a light and see what was on the other side. He was gone that quickly.

There have also been several waywards like this who have come to me at the home improvement store. The first one flipped through the flashlight bulbs I was stocking. I was rather amazed to catch this movement of the merchandise out of the corner of my eye. No one was around me at the time and it was late at night, near closing time. My shocked silence didn't last long.

"May I help you?" I asked.

"About damn time someone asked! I'm looking for some 5/8" plywood and need some help."

"No problem," I said as I began to walk toward lumber and felt the wayward follow me. "But this stuff here isn't what you want."

"Why not?"

Good grief, this man was pissed!

"Because this is the cheap stuff. The best plywood is on the other side of that light. See it?"

"Yes."

"There's a guy named Jerry on the other side of the light who can show you some really great plywood for very little money."

In my mind's eye, I could see a man on the other side, dressed in jeans and a casual shirt. I almost laughed out loud!

"Well, we'll see."

I walked into the light and the man followed. The queasy, nauseated feeling was almost overpowering, this being only the second time I'd walked through the tunnel, but the feeling quickly dissipated and I went about restocking the shelves again.

Pigeon Man

I took Colette to a local library one day. While she was busy on the Internet, I decided to take a walk in the neighborhood. I found some interesting old buildings and started looking around.

I always have liked birds, I thought to myself. *I miss the doves I used to raise.*

"I hate pigeons," I heard, loudly and clearly in my head. "They shit all over the place, even on people."

Rather shocked that I'd found a wayward on my walk, I thought for a moment. He sounded like an cranky old man.

"You could get away from them by going to the light," I thought, as strongly as I could.

"Are there pigeons there, too?"

"Yes, but they won't shit on your head."

I could feel amusement from the old man wayward, coming from my left.

"And if they do?" he said slowly, almost threateningly.

"You can come back and shit on my head."

"All right, you got yourself a deal."

I felt the tunnel of light open up and the old man leave. And no, no one has ever shit on my head!

Afterword

Sometimes crossing a wayward is just this easy. The people in these stories mentioned the light, and the ghost went to the other side. Sometimes that's all you really need to do: light a candle and say, "Go to the light." You may have to say it several times, but with you pushing from the physical side and the spirits on the other side pulling, the ghost will eventually cross.

These easy crossings show that you don't always have to "communicate" with the wayward or try to figure out what the ghost wants. We communicate with a lot of the waywards we meet because we have the ability, and a lot of them need to be convinced of something (as many of the stories in this book show). Some of you may have or may develop this ability; if so, use it to your full advantage. As I've said before, though, you just have to have the desire to help these poor, confused souls, and the determination to get them to where they need to go. Believe me, it's well worth the effort.

For me, working in retail, sometimes it takes very little effort to help a ghost to the other side. Most of the ones I've dealt with in the store, while I'm working, are ready to follow me when I lead them to a better product than any that can exist on this side of the veil. I have crossed several waywards this way.

One time at work, a customer saw me doing this. I'm not sure what, exactly, he saw, but the expression on his face was priceless! He seemed truly astounded as I came out of the tunnel. Whether he saw the light or just sensed that something special was going on, I'm not sure, but he definitely felt that something was different about the situation, or me, as he stood leaning on the counter of the Pro Desk watching me.

When crossing waywards, always start off by keeping things as simple as possible. Drama may be good for television and movies, but most of the time ghosts don't need tension and dramatics. My attitude toward "drama for drama's sake" is similar to my feelings about those who tease a wayward into performing tricks. These souls were once people, and we must remember to put ourselves in their position. Would we want to be teased until we started throwing things around? No!

Actually, I have run across one earthbound soul who was teasing *me*; I share this story later in the book. I tried to stay calm, but I did eventually lose my cool, so to speak (in ninety degree weather, it wasn't that hard to do). The ghost was teasing another wayward as well, but he did eventually cross when he became bored. Hey, just about anything can be done in the service of crossing a wayward!

Speaking of anything for the cause ... yes, I did tell the cranky old man wayward that he could shit on my head if he didn't like what was on the other side of the light. This was a lot like the agreement Colette made with a cranky old man who was attached to my flannel shirt (again, story to come!). Both ghosts have since crossed and come back to "visit," but not in a malicious way.

Not every crossing is serious! We do try to keep our sense of humor with this work, and that helps a lot. Yes, it is work, but it is very enjoyable work, and sometimes we are given the opportunity to laugh. If you don't laugh at yourself, who are you going to laugh at?

Candi's Mother-in-Law

"**M**y mother-in-law died five years ago," my friend Candi told me.

Nausea threatened to overtake me; I immediately knew the woman in question was wayward. But that was just the beginning. I waited calmly for Candi to continue, and swallowed hard.

She paused and took a drag from her cigarette, then put her blinker on and took the next exit off I-65. We were driving to Nashville to pick up her daughter.

"She's helping my soon-to-be-ex find me," Candi said.

The story of Candi actually started about six months earlier. Dwayne, who is Native American, and I used to vend at powwows (Native American festivals that showcase Native artists and their heritage), and on the way home from one I was dozing in the passenger seat next to him when I had a vision of a woman with long dark hair.

"I have to kill him before he kills me!" she yelled at me.

"You don't have to kill him," I told her. "You just have to get away from him."

"No! I have to kill him before he kills me!" she kept insisting.

I came out of this vision shaking with fear. After calming down for a few minutes, I told Dwayne about it.

About a month later, Dwayne came home from a powwow and told me about this couple he wanted me to meet. The next day was Sunday and I was off work. We went to the fairground where the festival was being held, and I met Candi and her partner.

After getting to know her for a few hours, I told her about the vision I'd had. She confirmed that she'd dyed her red hair dark brown at about that time, and that she still felt that way about her husband. "Shaken to the core" doesn't begin to describe how I felt; I knew I had been directed, in a big way, to meet her and become friends with her.

"Your husband knows his mother is wayward?" I asked Candi now, as we drove down a busy street in Nashville.

"Yes."

We pulled up the drive to the hotel and checked in. The accommodations were nice and we settled in quickly. I called Dwayne to let him know we'd arrived safely.

"So, what about your mother-in-law?" I asked after I'd gotten off my phone.

"She's with us now."

"So that's why I'm feeling nauseated," I said. It wasn't the same feeling I get when the tunnel opens near me; it was somehow a "sicker" feeling than that.

"Yeah, me too," she said. "He has enough psychic ability to understand her. I've barely been able to keep a step or two ahead of him, to keep him from finding me."

I immediately put up a blocking shield to keep our conversation private. What we were going to discuss did not need to go any farther. With the shield in place, Candi's mother-in-law would not be able to hear or sense our plan for how to cross her to the other side.

"Wow. Let me ask for help on this one," I said.

"Sure."

That night I prayed for help and received a dream. I was behind my house, inside the circle that Colette and Dwayne had built for our Wiccan ceremonies. The waist-high limestone altar had minimal tools on it: my athame, incense, a candle, blessed salt, and blessed water. I saw myself bless the space and draw up a circle. Then I drew up a second, then a third circle, each getting smaller until I was in the center of the smallest and next to the altar. I had never cast a circle like this one before, nor had I read or heard of such a circle.

Suddenly a small old woman flew into the largest circle. She was riding on a cornstalk, like a Halloween witch rides on a broomstick. She got off the cornstalk and used it as a walking staff, entering the first circle as if it wasn't there. She then walked through the second circle with the same ease, but the cornstalk bumped against the edge of the second circle. She tried to leave, but couldn't go back the way she had come. I knew she could not come into the third circle.

Next to me was a beautiful, Greek-looking woman. She was dressed in a Grecian-goddess dress. It was white and gold and started on one shoulder, spiraling down like a candy cane, wrapping around her body and ending in the middle of her thighs. I knew immediately she was my patron goddess, Hecate.

In the morning I told Candi about the dream. "Why would your mother-in-law have a cornstalk?"

"She was Cherokee, and corn is sacred to them. It's like your wand or staff is to you."

"Oh, a power thing—a directing thing."

"Yes."

"Now I understand that part," I said. "And I know that you and I are supposed to have a circle in my backyard, where you call her to us. She'll be able to come completely into the first circle, but her cornstalk won't be able to come through the second. She'll have to let go of it, or she won't be able to leave the second circle where you'll be. I'm going to be in the third circle where she can't get to me. I'm to invoke Hecate, my patron goddess. Then we'll cross her over."

I didn't think Candi totally understood the implications of what I was saying, but then she said, "I had a dream that we were in your bedroom and I was gathering things up in a hurry. You had this purple scarf that we were putting things into and we wrapped them in the scarf and hurried outside. Now the dream makes sense to me."

Since Candi had never seen my Wiccan tools, I was excited that she'd described some of them with enough detail that I knew we were getting massive help from the other side. Candi knew enough about her own Native heritage to accept that my being Wiccan was not a bad thing. This was the first inkling I had that this would be a very necessary and powerful crossing.

"It looks like we'll have some powerful help," I said. "Both of us getting information about this crossing means we'll be successful."

"Sounds like we have a good plan."

"Don't say anything to anyone. We're going to play this one close to our hearts, to keep your mother-in-law in the dark about all this."

"Yeah; if she gets any idea about this, she won't come."

A couple of days later was the full moon. It had been raining, with lightning strikes all over town. I knew that this would be the first time in a long while that I would need that kind of power. It kept me on my toes whenever I felt Candi's mother-in-law around; I temporarily blocked down my psychic center and tried to appear nonthreatening.

"She's a small woman," I stated.

"Yes, but don't let that fool you; she's very powerful," Candi told me.

"Oh, yeah," I said, and paused. "My great-grandmother's name was Ida Pearl, but I keep hearing Ida Mae. My great-grandma was half Native."

"Ida Mae was my mother-in-law's name," Candi said.

There was an extended silence between us.

"I'm a little nervous."

"Yeah, me too," Candi said.

That evening we went shopping for our after-circle grounding food. We bought a bottle of wine, root veggies like carrots and potato salad, and some cheese and crackers. At the supermarket we saw Colette's friend, Olivia. She wanted to know what we were buying the snacks for, and we told her. Colette was still away at college, but Olivia wanted to join in and help. Three is a good number, so we invited her to join us.

The rain slacked off as we all pulled into my driveway, but I was still a little concerned about the overcast sky and cloud-to-cloud lightning.

"Should we wait? Try this another time?" Candi asked.

I thought about it, briefly.

"No, we're going to need the divine help that's offered to us. We'll be protected."

The three of us slogged through the wet grass behind my house, each carrying something for the ceremony. Candi had some of my tools wrapped in my purple scarf, just like she'd seen in her dream. I had massive butterflies in my stomach at the thought of what we were about to do. I had directed and participated in many circles before, mostly by myself, being a solitary Wiccan. They were all different, but this one seemed destined to be outstanding.

We weren't disappointed.

I cleared and blessed my holy ground. My nervousness began to dissipate as I drew up the first circle. I took my athame and called the four quarters, then directed Candi and Olivia to move closer to the altar. I drew the second circle around us. The third circle I drew up around myself and the altar; then I raised my eyes and arms skyward.

"Hecate, Triple Goddess of the Crossroads, hear my call. I invite you to this circle to help us in our quest." I realized that my anxiety was gone now, replaced by pure energy. "I invoke you tonight!"

With all my powers of concentration, I imagined a white swirling light approaching me, centering over me, then dropping down into my body. I felt light-headed and very calm, but still in total control of my physical being.

"Candi," I said, my voice sounding slightly different—softer, maybe. "Call your mother-in-law to this circle."

"Ida Mae, come to us now. We have something to discuss with you!" Candi commanded.

We waited, but no mother-in-law appeared. I nodded to Candi to try again.

"Ida Mae, I need to talk to you! Come to me now!" She almost yelled the order.

I saw the small old woman, in my mind's eye, flying in. She stopped at the edge of the first circle to get off her cornstalk, and walked purposefully in. Then she walked into the second circle. The cornstalk stopped. She glared at the three of us and tried to exit the circles, but the second one wouldn't let her go back out the way she had come in. Candi saw the same thing I did.

"You have to let go of your cornstalk," Candi said.

The old woman tried several more times to pull the cornstalk through the second circle, but it just bumped against the force field. Again, she glared at all of us, and eventually let go of her prize. It dissolved into the ground.

"You have to go to the light, Mother Ida Mae."

I could feel that Candi's fear of the old woman was giving Ida Mae courage. Hecate directed our energies toward my friend.

The wayward didn't speak, choosing instead to shake her fist in Candi's face. The old woman had a lot of power and anger. A brief feeling of fear entered my mind about what the wayward might be able to do with all this power, but it quickly dissipated. Somehow we were all protected, and I almost laughed at the silliness of my fears. Hecate and God were a lot stronger than this ghost.

Several spirits then showed up from the other side. They looked like her relatives, and included Injun Joe (from the story in the previous chapter) and my own great-grandmother, Ida Pearl. They surrounded Candi's mother-in-law with the pink light of love, and she calmed down dramatically.

"Go with them to the light, Ida Mae. You know that's where you belong," I said. I could hear Hecate's soft but authoritative voice speaking through me.

The tunnel of light formed between the first and second circles; we all waited expectantly, maybe even a little anxiously. A full minute passed before the tension totally evaporated and Ida Mae and friends went through the tunnel. We all were silent for a few moments, enjoying the lingering, peaceful sensations of the pink light.

"Hecate, I release you from the physical. Go with my love, gratitude, and peace," I said as I again raised my arms and saw the

93

white light leave me. I felt somewhat empty afterward, but filled with love at the same time.

I took down the circle around me, then the one around Candi and Olivia.

"I leave a gift of cakes and ale for the spirits who have helped us this night," I said as I put our offering, a cookie and a small glass of wine, on the ground at the edge of the first circle. Then I dismissed the quarters and pulled up the last circle.

"Merry we meet and merry we part until merry we meet again," I said, as a thank you to the spirits.

"Wow," said Olivia. "That was incredible!"

"What?" I asked.

"When you called Hecate, I saw lightning nearby, and then a light go into you."

"Really?" I asked, astounded. Colette and I had come to accept these kinds of things, but Olivia had never seen them before.

"I saw it, too," Candi agreed. "And when you dismissed her, there was lightning again."

"And I saw an old woman go into a light!" Olivia almost squealed. "That was just too cool!"

Their excitement about the ceremony quickly rubbed off on me as we gathered my Wiccan tools and went inside to ground with food and wine. It was already well past dark, and it took several more hours before we finally began to calm down from the ceremony. I was so glad to have shared that special time with my friends.

Candi was never bothered again by her now ex-mother-in-law.

Afterword

Injun Joe, from the last chapter, was crossed just before I helped Candi with her mother-in-law. Since both Injun Joe and Ida Mae were Native Americans from the same area, we were pretty sure they were related. Injun Joe returned to help cross Ida Mae.

This was the most dramatic crossing I'd been a part of in my work so far, and also the most powerful because of the energies that were needed to cross the wayward involved. As I'm sure you've already noticed, I usually try to stay away from drama when crossing a wayward. For the most part, when drama is involved, the people inciting the drama tend to go overboard, and that's not always a good thing. In this case, however, the dramatics helped me to raise my vibrations to a level above that of Ida Mae's vibrations, which was what was needed in order to cross her. I had to show her that I had power and knew how to use it—in a gentle way. That's why she didn't try too hard to mess things up. She was smart enough to realize that I was stronger than she was.

When I prepare for a circle, or Wiccan ceremony, I fast for a few hours beforehand. This tends to raise spiritual vibrations. Catholics used to fast for at least an hour before going to church so that they could take the sacrament of Communion. I also have a routine of taking a ritual bath, to cleanse all negativity from my physical body. Then I dress in my Wiccan regalia: a handmade robe and a special belt, a special, double-edged knife called an athame, and usually a wand. All of these things will prepare me for casting a circle and raising my vibrations to a higher level.

I take a Wiccan ceremony seriously; it's like going to church. You clean up and dress in your "Sunday best," as they used to say. Then you're ready to listen to what the priest or preacher has to say. The robe, athame, and wand, along with incense and candles, are all a part of getting into the drama of the ceremony. They are not necessary for the ceremony, but they help you to get into the right frame of mind, much like showering and getting dressed up for church. They signal the mind and body that something special is going to happen and that you need to be prepared for it.

All of us had something to learn from crossing Ida Mae. I learned more about my own power and how to tap into the God-given energy around me. This is what attracted me to Witchcraft in the first place. Since I've been practicing Wicca, I've learned about different energies and which ones can be used for good things and which ones I can do no more than neutralize for now. Some energies I can only repel, and "let go and let God." This is what I believe Wicca is all about—changing bad to good where we can. Yes, there are some out in the world who use these energies for their own purposes, but that will eventually catch up to them.

Crossing Ida Mae was the first and only time, so far, that I have had to use so much protection when crossing an earthbound soul. And I don't, as a rule, use my religion to cross waywards. Ghosts retain memories of their most recent life the most clearly, and since there was so much prejudice against witches during recent centuries, I feel that using Witchcraft as a means of crossing waywards is more of a hindrance than a help. Nevertheless, I was guided to do this particular crossing in this manner. Ida Mae needed to see that I had more power than she did; I was protecting Candi and Olivia as well as myself. I know that Ida Mae could see all the protection I had erected around us, as well as Hecate within me. She was spiritually aware enough that these sights made an impression on her, so she didn't try to harm us. Ida Mae was a very dangerous earthbound soul; all these precautions needed to be taken in order for us to be protected from her energy, and for the crossing to be successful.

I occasionally invoke Hecate to help me with my energy work in general. Let me explain a little about *invoking*. This is when one calls on energy (preferably a good energy, or at least a neutral energy that is used for good) and allows that energy to descend into the physical world. Precautions need to be taken—when invoking, you are quite vulnerable, and your physical self needs to be protected. I always make sure I'm within sacred space; in other words, I make sure that I have barriers up that protect me from unwanted energies. For the Ida Mae crossing, I was allowing energy to enter my physical body in a way that most people would not consider "normal"; instead of eating food for energy, I was directing energy into my body spiritually.

I do not recommend invoking unless you know what you are doing. I have been studying Wicca for over two decades now, and have invoked this kind of energy only a few times, and only for special occasions. There are plenty of good books if you want to learn more about this process; see the suggested reading list at the back of this book.

To a lot of people, the concept of invoking is quite foreign and frightening, but remember that invoking is not the same thing as possession. I was in control of my physical body, although I did feel different, like there was some directing of my physical being going on that was not of my own volition. I do not believe that you can actually be possessed unless there is an agreement. Either we plan it while on the other side, before this lifetime, or we choose to allow it, consciously or unconsciously, after we come into the physical world. The difference in what I did and what most people consider *possession* is that I was in control of the energy and what my physical body was doing. I asked Hecate to enter me and then I asked her to leave, and that's what happened. I respect my patron goddess, and she respects me.

Hecate is a powerful energy. When I first became aware of her and her power, it did make me a little wary. Being a solitary practitioner for almost the whole time I'd been Wiccan, I hadn't put much thought into a patron goddess before she began to work with me. At the same time, I knew that I would not have planned something that I wasn't able to deal with. I have faith in my own abilities and intelligence. I knew that I would not have chosen to work with such a powerful force if I couldn't handle the consequences. There are always consequences, good and/or bad. For the most part, I feel that Hecate chose me, but I always had the free-will choice not to work with her.

Hecate is a triple goddess. She embodies all three phases of a woman: the maiden, the mother, and the crone. The maiden is a young woman; she has started her menses, but not yet become pregnant. She carries the youthful vibrancy that comes with that stage of life. The mother is the nurturing and protective aspect of the feminine. The crone is a menopausal or post-menopausal woman who has acquired the wisdom of age. Hecate is also a goddess of the crossroads, of choices. Of course, there is a lot more to her than I can include in this brief summary, but you can do more research if you choose.

Ida Mae, I believe, consciously chose to go wayward. This, I have discovered while doing this work, is exceedingly rare. When a person dies and sees the light, she either goes to it (consciously or unconsciously) or has some sort of distraction and avoids it, either because of fear or due to a desire to complete some unfinished business. These are, by far, the most common reasons why deceased souls go wayward.

From participating in this crossing, Candi learned that she had the ability to deal with a spiritually powerful soul. Candi and Olivia both needed to see that this kind of power is real, and then verify it with me and with each other. Overall, it was a work of art on the part of Mom and Dad.

For her part, Olivia needed to see that there are many aspects and dimensions to spiritual work. She was rather young but she'd had some psychic experiences, and this ceremony added to her wisdom in these matters.

When the need arises, we can accomplish miracles—sometimes with Mom and Dad's help, sometimes by ourselves. I firmly believe this, and the experience with Ida Mae helped to bolster my beliefs even more.

Our Favorite Ghost Stories

Some ghost stories are just too good not to share. What follows are a few tales of unusual interactions with waywards that happened over a time span of several years. Each one is instructive in its own way!

There's a Ghost Attached to My Shirt

"This shirt smells of mothballs," I told Colette as I folded the freshly laundered red, white, and blue flannel shirt. "It always has."

"You're right," she said, sniffing the shirt. "Why?"

"I'm not sure," I said thoughtfully. "I've had it for over four years now and I've done everything I can think of to get the smell out. I've washed it in perfumed laundry detergent. I've hung it outside on the clothesline. I've sprayed it with that clothes deodorant stuff. Hell … I've even sprayed perfume on it, and it still smells of mothballs!"

Colette took the shirt from me and held it for a few seconds, then smiled.

"It has a wayward attached to it," she said, and giggled.

"Good grief!"

"That's not the best part."

I eyed my seventeen-year-old suspiciously. "What?"

"He died wearing this shirt. It was his favorite."

"Great. Where is he?"

"In the same town where Mrs. Walton lived."

"I got this shirt at one of the Goodwill stores there."

"Makes sense to me," Colette said. She shrugged and walked away.

So, despite being eighty miles away from that town, we made plans to go there, cross the wayward, and also look for jobs. I was recently divorced and needed income, so we'd decided to move nearer to a city where we could support ourselves. The greater Lexington area seemed like a pretty good choice, if we could find jobs.

The town was only a few miles away from Lexington and somewhat small, so we were able to find the earthbound soul without too much trouble. Colette was able to zero in on him, and directed me to park on the side of the road near some modest houses.

"He won't go," Colette announced, after about ten minutes.

"Argue with him, baby. You can argue the fuzz off a peach."

She grinned, and concentrated again.

"Okay," she said, smiling.

"What happened?" I asked, starting the van and pulling away from the curb.

"I told him if he didn't like it on the other side, he could come back and haunt us."

All I could do was roll my eyes at her tenacious, quick-thinking mind. I pulled into traffic.

The Woman Who Wanted Revenge ... Again

"There's a wayward across the street," Colette said one day, as we pulled into the local McDonald's drive-through.

"Great. How many waywards can this town have?" We'd already found three others (not mentioned in this book) and crossed them.

"We have some astrals who want to help cross her."

"Let's see what's up, first," I said, sensing something overtly obstinate about this one.

"She killed her husband and the woman she caught him with, then herself," Colette informed me.

"Did the other two cross?"

"Yes."

"I can feel her hostility. Be careful. And I don't want the astrals getting too close to the light."

It was early spring, another gray, dreary, blustery day. I watched my daughter cross the street as I continued through the drive-through and ordered our lunch. We were on a tight schedule, but I had confidence that Colette would be able to cross her earthbound soul quickly.

A few minutes later, I saw her come back across the road.

"Did y'all get her crossed? Are all the astrals still here?"

"No and yes."

"What's the problem?"

"She still wants to kill her husband. Again."

All I could do was stare at my daughter in shock.

"She thinks that she survived the murder/suicide, and that he did too. She wants to kill him. We got her to come over to the sidewalk in front of the van."

"She can't be that stupid—" I began, but Colette's glare stopped me short. "All right."

We sat thinking for a few minutes, eating our lunch in the van. We were both determined not to leave this woman wayward.

"Okay, let her kill him again."

"What?" Colette said, nearly choking on her fries.

"Get her all pumped up. Say, 'You really want to hurt him for what he did to you,' and so on. Then make an astral gun and tell her to go get him. The ones on the other side will take care of her when she goes through the tunnel."

I could see Colette mulling over the idea for a few seconds.

"It could work."

Taking another bite of my sandwich, I concentrated. My energy was low, but I could feel the tension and excitement coming from the sidewalk in front of the van. In a flash I saw one of our astral friends hand the woman a "gun," and she ran through the tunnel. I saw several spirits from home tackle the woman. The gun evaporated, and I laughed. I looked over at Colette, to see her in a full belly roll as well.

"What happened?" I asked. I wanted to find out if she would confirm what I'd seen in my vision. She did, and we laughed even harder.

God Is Calling My Name!

Sometimes people come to me with dreams and want me to interpret them. I sort of have a reputation among my coworkers as being a little strange that way. One day, Cheryl, a cashier and fellow Wiccan, called me over and told me about her dream. In it, three people who said that they were dead approached her, each one taking his or her turn. Cheryl pointed them all to a house that was very brightly lit, and they went to it.

"It was such a strange dream—what does it mean?"

"Do you dream in color?" I asked, straightening the shelves on the register cap.

"Sometimes."

"Was this dream in color?"

Cheryl thought about it for a minute. "Yes, I think it was in color."

"It looks like you're going to cross three waywards to the light."

"Oh, I don't think so. I've never crossed waywards!"

"It's not so hard to do. I'll help you."

A few days later, I felt the first of her waywards around her and told her so. She refused to cross him over, but I did get her to tune in to what the wayward wanted and what he looked like. I was trying to get her used to using her psychic abilities. Maybe I could get her to cross the next one.

Cheryl refused to cross the second wayward as well, so I ended up crossing both of them. The third was the hardest, and rather than arguing with Cheryl again about learning how to cross waywards, I decided just to do it myself.

The third wayward told me that his wife had poisoned him. I could feel his depression over the situation and tried for three days to cross him. Nothing I said made him feel good enough to cross over. His main problem was that he didn't believe in God.

On the third day of arguing with this wayward, I had to get off the floor. Between the wayward, my chauvinistic supervisor, and cranky customers, I felt like I wanted to start cussing everyone I saw. Instead of getting fired for verbally abusing customers and coworkers, I decided to take a smoke break.

At first I just sat down on some concrete blocks outside and tried to calm down. I began chanting softly to myself: "AhhhOmmmm."

"What are you doing?" I heard the wayward ask.

"I'm grounding and centering myself," I said, continuing to chant and calm down. "It makes me feel better."

"I like the way it makes me feel."

It suddenly clicked. This was how I was to help this earth-bound soul connect with God! "You would like the way the light feels as well," I said.

"I can't go," he replied.

"Why not?"

"Because God forgot about me."

"God never forgets about any of us. We only push him away from us and feel empty because of that." I lit a cigarette.

"God doesn't even know my name."

"Yes he does. When you're ready to go home, he'll call your name."

"I don't think so."

"Why don't you try chanting? It would help you feel better."

In my mind, I heard him begin to chant as I had. Suddenly he stopped.

"What's wrong?" I asked.

"Someone is calling me," the earthbound soul said.

I could feel his uncertainty, and then I felt immense love flood the area in front of the store.

"It's God," I said with a smile.

"God, is that you?" I heard the wayward say.

I grinned broadly as I felt a sudden, massive surge of love. It was an ecstasy like I'd never felt before: pure love from our parents!

"It *is* God! He's calling my name!"

The wayward started jumping up and down in his excitement. It filled me with such happiness that I started crying. This was the first, and so far only, wayward I have cried over. He ran into the tunnel.

"Thank you!" The words were so loud in my mind that I had to look around to see if anyone else had heard them. "Thank you! Thank you!" The words just kept repeating in my mind as tears flowed down my cheeks.

Who Fed Socrates Cheez-Its?

We walked into the Nashville hotel room, bags in hand.

"I want this one," Colette said as she put her bags down on the bed next to the window.

"Cool. Dwayne and I will take this one," I said. I knew Dwayne would want to watch television until early in the morning, and the volume could be kept lower if we took the bed nearest the TV.

Colette let her five-pound Chihuahua out of his crate. He began running around, sniffing at the smells in our temporary new home.

"You want a Cheez-It, Sock Rat?" Dwayne asked, offering the cracker to Socrates.

The tiny dog's eyes bugged out even more as he ran up to Dwayne and gently took the offered tidbit.

"We have cable!" Dwayne sat on the bed with remote in hand and began flipping through the channels; Socrates sat next to him and began munching on the cracker.

After we'd settled in, we decided to get dinner. Dwayne left the television on to keep the dog company. When we came back, he noticed that the TV had been turned off.

"What happened to the TV?" He began searching for the remote.

"What do you mean?" I asked.

"I left it on to keep Socrates calm, and now it's off. And I can't find the remote."

"Here it is." Colette picked it up off the air conditioner under the window.

"But I left it on the bed."

"Maybe the maid came in," I suggested.

"This late in the day?"

"I don't know." I looked at Colette. "Do you feel any waywards around?"

"No."

"Neither do I."

After our experience with my ex-husband's attitude toward our spiritual work, Colette and I at first tended not to tell Dwayne a lot about our wayward wrangling or other psychic experiences. By now, though, we'd realized that Dwayne was a lot more accepting—not only about the ghosty things, but about other things as well. We were becoming more open about our spirituality and beliefs around him, and this wayward would prove to be a sort of turning point for the three of us.

That night, Dwayne and I slept hard, but Colette had a problem. She told us about it in the morning.

"There was a man in here last night," she started, as we dressed to go downstairs for the continental breakfast. "I think he's a wayward."

"But we didn't feel him yesterday or last night."

"I know. But I woke up sometime during the night and saw him standing by the window. I think he put the remote there yesterday."

"What did he look like?"

"He was as tall as Dwayne and kind of thin. He had long hair."

I looked out the window. In a small area between the roofs of the buildings, I could see a field. This field could only be seen if you stood at the end of the air conditioning unit that was nearest the bed.

"Was he standing in the corner, or closer to your bed?"

"To my bed."

The wayward had obviously been looking at the field as he stood by the window. It was the only thing of interest to see.

"Could he have been Native?" I asked, feeling a strong need to be outside in that field.

"Probably."

"Where is he now?"

"I'm not sure."

"It's just strange that neither of us can feel him around."

"Yeah."

That night, we attended Colette's college graduation ceremony. It was hot—the middle of July—and we were all sweating throughout most of the event. We were so very proud of her as she walked up to the podium to receive her diploma in her cap and gown. Afterwards, we went out to celebrate.

When we got back to the hotel, we noticed a small pile of Cheez-Its on Colette's bed. Socrates was proudly sitting beside his treasure and wagging his spastic little tail.

"Who fed Socrates Cheez-Its?" Dwayne asked as he picked up one of the crackers. Socrates' eyes bugged out and he began stalking the cracker in Dwayne's fingers.

"You didn't leave them for him?" I asked, as the dog gently took the cracker and ran back to guard the pile.

"No, and the box is still on the dresser where I left it. It's still closed up."

"I think your friend is back, Colette." I giggled and then sang: "UuuWEEEuuu!"

"I think it's a little creepy that neither of us can feel him around," Colette said.

"The weather's rather dry … has been for several weeks, and we're not near any water to speak of. Humidity helps us to connect with waywards better, even if they're trying to hide from us."

The rest of the trip was uneventful; neither of us was able to talk the ghost over. He didn't say much to us, either, and we had grown a little frustrated with him.

When we got back to Kentucky, I decided to mow the lawn. It had been a couple of weeks since I'd given the lawn a haircut and even with the dry weather, it still needed to be done.

In the backyard, I began feeling the wayward from the hotel in Nashville. He seemed quite amused that we had an altar set up.

"Do you make sacrifices on your altar?" I heard him ask, after I'd told him the very basics of what I used it for.

"No, don't be stupid!" I said, the heat irritating me as much as his question. I could sense that he knew better but was trying to get a rise out of me.

"Why else would you have a rock table behind your house?"

"Because I want to," I said, rather perturbed that the wayward hadn't crossed even though Colette and I had both tried. It was over ninety degrees and just after noon; all I wanted to do was finish the lawn and go inside where it was cool. "Listen, if you want to find out more about me, go to the light and you can look up anything you want to know. It's all over there."

"Heathen!" I heard.

"What? What did you call me?"

"Heathen! You're going to burn in hell!"

"Who are *you*?" I asked, sensing energy much different than the Native American I'd been dealing with.

"You are a sinner!"

I could feel the first wayward's amusement. How I'd attracted another wayward, who thought I was going to hell, was beyond me. Trying hard, I was able to see a man with an old-fashioned, wide-brimmed black hat on. His black jacket hung down to his knees. A white shirt, one of those black string ties, and black pants completed his hellfire-and-brimstone preacher look, complete with a tattered Bible that he clutched to his chest like a protective shield. I could feel his fear of me. At the same time, he was determined to send me back to the hell I came from.

I have a button that says, *God, please save me from your fan club*, and boy, I sure needed saving just then!

"Look, 'Injun Joe,' just go to the light and leave me alone," I said as I wiped sweat from my eyes. He hadn't told me his name, so in my irritation I called him the first thing that came to mind, secretly hoping it would insult him and he would go home. "And take your friend with you!"

Laughter filled my head.

"I like you. You're funny."

"You're a heathen too!"

"Maybe," the Native American said.

"Do you believe in God? The One True Christian God?" the preacher asked, thumping his Bible with one hand while holding it out to the Native with the other.

"Maybe."

If I hadn't been so irritated with the two of them as well as the heat, I probably would have laughed out loud.

"You will burn in hell if you do not accept the One True God as your only God!"

"I believe in the Great Spirit."

"That is not God!"

"Sure he is."

"Have you been saved by someone like me? Have you accepted God into your life?"

"Maybe."

"The gates of heaven shall be closed to all who do not accept God as their savior!" the preacher yelled, thumping his Bible again.

"Can you guys take this elsewhere?" I asked, wiping sweat from my face again.

"I find this amusing," I felt the Native say; I could almost see the grin on his face.

"Glad *you* do."

Laughter again.

"You are both going to burn in hell!"

"Yeah, well, I already know that hell doesn't want me there and heaven isn't ready for me yet. You two, on the other hand, both need to cross over and leave me the hell alone."

If the Native had been physical, he would have died from laughter.

"Heathen! You are in league with the devil! God will strike you down!"

"I don't believe in your devil," I quipped, irritated.

"You are going to hell if you don't accept God into your life!"

"You sure have a one-track mind," I said as I turned the mower down another row. I began to wonder if the preacher had died of a heart attack, given his type-A personality.

"You seem to be pretty one-track as well," the Native American said, drawing himself back into the argument.

"Lord, God Almighty, please help me to save these doomed souls," the preacher said as he knelt and held his Bible skyward.

I laughed out loud. Here was an earthbound soul trying to save me so I could go to heaven!

Somehow I put up with the hellfire-and-brimstone preacher wayward and the Native wayward arguing with each other for almost an hour as I mowed the back lawn in the heat of that late July day, sweating profusely the whole time. Finally, the Native grew tired of the preacher and went through the tunnel to the other side. Thank you, God!

"You're a heathen! You'll burn in hell for what you do! You do the devil's work! God is going to strike you down!"

"You know what? I've got a daughter inside that house who's more of a heathen than I am—go argue with her for a while!"

I felt the preacher leave, and I was finally able to finish the lawn in peace.

Poetic Justice

This is the next episode in the story of the hellfire-and-brimstone preacher, as told to me by Colette.

She was in her bedroom, gathering material and patterns together so she could take them to a friend who wanted some clothes made. (Colette had gone to school for fashion design.)

"Are you the heathen?" She heard the question suddenly.

"What are you talking about?" she asked; she was unaware that I'd sent the preacher to her.

"Are you the one who does the devil's work?" This question was asked in a stronger way.

"What the hell are you talking about?"

"You live in this house and have a heathen altar in the back!" he said accusingly. "You and your mother worship the devil!"

"Good God, what do you want?" Colette asked, realizing she was dealing with a wayward preacher. She could see that his black clothes looked burned, and they were smoking as he stood before her.

"How dare you take the Lord's name in vain! God will strike you down for that!"

"What the hell is your problem?"

"Blasphemy! You're going to go to hell! You're a heathen!"

"Kiss my ass!"

"Blasphemy! God will—"

"Yeah, yeah, I know," she began, then clutched at her chest and began to gasp.

"I told you! God is going to strike you down!"

"Not really, I just wanted to have some fun," Colette said as she straightened and giggled. Then she heaved a sigh; she knew she would not be able to accomplish much until she crossed this very distracting ghost. Concentrating, she began to pull information forward about the preacher.

There was a small, wooden church in a wooded area near a few other small wooden houses. It seemed to be around the turn of the nineteenth century. The preacher was in the church, preaching at the pulpit. After the sermon, the congregation left, then he left. Black clouds had gathered during the church service and lightning lit up the sky as he began walking home. He reached the top of a hill and stopped under a large tree as the rain began to pelt him. That's when lightning struck the tree, tossing him several yards away. He lay still and his clothes were smoking. Colette came out of the vision laughing.

"What is your problem, heathen?"

"You got what you deserved!"

"What are you talking about?"

"Look," she said, getting down to business. "There's a church on the other side of that light. They really need you to preach to them. They're lost without their preacher. He ran away because they were such heathens."

"Why should I believe what the devil's child says?"

"Because I just came from that church; now they all need saving!"

The preacher seemed to be thinking about what Colette said. What if she had just come from the church? Those people needed to be saved from her evil influence! The tunnel of light opened up and the preacher ran though it—to save the heathen-infested church!

Afterword

As I've mentioned before, not all of our wayward wrangling is serious stuff. Sometimes it's humorous, which makes it easier to handle the difficult and serious ghosts. Don't get me wrong—this work is very serious, but it's nice to be able to laugh when a situation presents itself, as it did in the stories told here.

Yes, I still have the shirt that the cranky wayward was attached to, and I still wear it. Hey, it's a nice warm shirt! That was one of the times we found we could challenge a ghost into going home. We don't do this a lot, but when the situation calls for it, it's in our bag of tricks.

With this book, I'm hoping to show that there are a variety of different ways in which earthbound souls can be convinced to go home. Some are quick to cross, but many other times Colette and I need to expend a lot of energy—the wayward has to be persuaded to use free-will choice to go home. As I said before, it takes pushing from our physical dimension (where we belong) and pulling from the other side (where they belong) to accomplish this feat. The spirits on the other side want these souls to come back home—their friends and pets there miss them and want to be reunited with them. That is what the afterlife is all about.

My daughter has been extremely helpful to me in this special work, because while I have never been wayward after a physical lifetime, she has. I don't fully understand why someone would not want to go back to where there is perfect love and peace, where everything is … well … perfect. I have come to something of an understanding of this through dealing with these confused and sometimes tortured souls. There are times, however, like with the cranky ghost attached to my flannel shirt, that the need for the soul to stay earthbound escapes me.

Another example of this puzzling attachment to our world was a man who drowned in a lake near our house. As a wayward, he just wanted to keep fishing. Excuse me, but if you could fish in a perfect lake (stream, river, whatever), why would you want to stay where the water is polluted? Where some of the people around the lake straight-line their sewer into it instead of building a septic system? Where the cows and other farm animals swim and excrete into the water? It took a while to convince this soul to go with our friend from the other side to a perfect fishing hole. The whole situation astounded me. I just don't understand how people can get so attached to physical things that they go wayward just to continue "possession" of the physical object. The object is on the other side as well, and it is perfect there!

The second story in this chapter is about the woman who wanted revenge. She was so caught up in her desire for revenge that she refused to go to the light. She was bound and determined not to cross, so we convinced her she could exact her revenge again. I feel slightly conflicted about this strategy because we did tell a little fib; she would not succeed in getting revenge again. At the same time, she was so malicious about her situation that I felt the fib was justified. She has a lot to learn about justice and forgiveness, and I hope the love of the other side will help her to learn this valuable lesson.

In the third story, of the wayward who didn't believe that God wanted him, the issue could also have been revenge, but was actually a problem with belief. I felt that the man would have liked to get back at his wife for poisoning him, but the bottom line was that he felt God had abandoned him. This thought probably was present long before he died, and he had to feel the tremendous love that God—our parents—has for us before he felt he could cross. I felt that love too … and it was good for both of us, because, at that point in time, I really needed that little reminder. I guess we all do occasionally.

We know that God never abandons us. When we go through difficult times, our Mom and Dad are with us even more than before, giving us love and sending us help. I have seen this too many times in my own life, as well as in others' lives, to doubt it. By the same token, God allows us to stumble along on our own so we can learn our lessons. If Mom and Dad helped us up every time we fell, we would not learn to stand on our own. God is the perfect parent.

The stories about the Native and the preacher are so much a part of each other that it is a little difficult to find the separation point. Somehow Colette and I had picked up two very different types of ghosts, and had to deal with both of them at once. We never did figure out if the preacher first found us in Tennessee or whether he just appeared once we were back in Kentucky. Not that it really matters....

I try not to get upset with the lost souls I deal with. I try hard to give them comfort and understanding. With those two ghosts, however, it was very difficult for me to keep my calm. The Native American seemed to enjoy teasing and hiding from us. It wasn't that Colette and I weren't in the right frame of mind or that we couldn't raise our vibrations enough—I really believe he was trying to mask his presence. I guess he was tired of physical people ignoring him and decided to have fun with the two of us because we could sense him. Maybe it was the hot, dry weather that summer, or maybe he had recently learned how to hide from people. Either way, Colette and I were both a little frustrated with the Native and his hide-and-seek game.

I know the Native wayward wasn't shy, because he really enjoyed teasing me while I was mowing the backyard. And of course, he seemed to enjoy arguing with the preacher as well. I think he was just one of those people who like pushing others' buttons. Colette pretty much ignored him, so she wasn't any fun for him, but I tried to cross him. When I didn't react to his teasing after a while, he turned his attention to the preacher and had fun with him for quite some time, much to my dismay. It was only after he tired of getting a rise out of the preacher that he finally left. The preacher was so focused on his favorite topic that the Native man had a hard time getting him to switch tactics or topics long enough to make it interesting.

In general, the preacher was more difficult for Colette and I to deal with because we've both experienced well-intentioned Christians

117

in the physical world trying to save our souls. This became old years ago, but we still deal with it on a regular basis. We have no intention of changing our religion or belief system just because someone who doesn't know us thinks we should... would you?

I truly do not advocate arguing with earthbound souls—it tends to upset them, which makes them more difficult to cross. However, in this case, both waywards seemed to want to argue with us. Maybe that's what they needed to get themselves into the right frame of mind to cross over. I don't know, and it really doesn't matter. Each case is different. Each wayward is an individual, and that's the way to approach this job. For the most part, if you are able to learn at least a little information about them, then you have to figure out what to do with that information and what it is that the wayward really wants. Not a lot of waywards think logically when they first appear, and some never do. The main thing is that they eventually cross. If you have to argue with them, then do it!

Elizabeth

"What am I doing here?" she asked, after arriving late one night.

Her dark hair was pulled back from her face and curled softly against the collar of her black dress. The dress fit every curve of her body beautifully. There was a slit up the back of the straight, snug-fitting skirt, so that walking would be more comfortable. This wayward looked like she'd come straight out of a 1940s movie.

I had been path-walking, a form of meditation that leads you into a tranquil state. You visualize some sort of transition image (like a bridge, door, or rainbow) which goes to where you want to go; then you cross it (or, in the case of a door, go through it). Usually, the path-walking Colette and I do is for our own benefit.

We can remember past lives this way, or accomplish other things like breaking a bad habit or meeting with a spirit guide or totem animal. I had tried path-walking with a couple of earthbound souls before (which was how I found Marcella, my second commitment), and it had worked out well. As it did this time.

In my path-walking, I crossed a bridge and went through the door at the end of the bridge to where Elizabeth was. I then pulled her to me by concentrating on seeing her coming closer and closer. I led her back through the door and back over the bridge. "You're in my home. You're safe here," I told her.

"Why am I here?"

"Because you want something. What do you want?"

I could feel her pause, deep in thought. Whether it was the energy I was blasting toward her or the fact that I was just tired, I was beginning to feel a little loopy, like I was in a slow-motion dream.

"I want people to notice me. I've had people like you notice me, but they try to tell me I'm dead. I'm not dead!"

People like me. She seemed to assume I was a medium. Unlike mediums, I deal with ghosts, not spirits who have actually crossed. But she had a point; not everyone can see, hear, or feel waywards and their specific needs like Colette and I do.

"Okay," I said, and paused, trying to keep her calm. "You know that there are people on the other side who would really pay attention to you."

"I don't know that!" she practically yelled, in a perturbed and flippant manner.

That jerked me out of the calm, dreamlike state I was enjoying. Her irritation was already shooting through me. I knew I could irritate her more if I chose to, although I rarely resort to that tactic.

"Sure you do. I know you're smart enough to know I'm telling you the truth." I spoke calmly, trying to regain my own composure.

The wayward's stubbornness was palatable; she was going to fight me tooth and nail. I was ready. I had come across stubborn and even cranky waywards far ruder than she was proving to be. She was already angry with me, but for some reason she seemed to be holding back the biggest part of her anger. This anger would be a problem if she didn't release it in a constructive way, but I suspected it had to do with her disbelief that she had died, and her expectation that I was going to try to convince that her she had.

I knew about this wayward—her name was Elizabeth. I also knew that other people with psychic abilities had tried to cross her but were unsuccessful. Elizabeth confirmed that she'd been encouraged to go to the light before, but again flat-out denied that she was dead. She felt as physical as anyone else. Her belief was not shaken by questions like, "When was the last time you had something to eat or drink?" (even though not eating in sixty years could be considered a sure sign of physical death). Elizabeth was the most obstinate wayward I'd met in a long time.

For the most part, Colette and I don't worry much about how, when, or why a ghost's physical body died. But I knew, from an article I'd read, that Elizabeth had been murdered and cut in half; her body was later found in a field. I had been fascinated and disturbed by this story as soon as I read it. Finally, I'd felt the need to path-walk to learn more about this woman. And when I realized she was wayward, I knew that I had to help her, any way I could. And then I realized something else. For years, I'd been aware that my last commitment was in California, but I could never figure out a way of getting out there. Now, with the help of my path-walking, I not only knew who my commitment was, but I was able to bring her to me.

I let her stew for a while in my living room.

"Why can't I leave?" she asked, finally.

"Because you don't really want to," I said, trying to re-create that dreamlike calm I'd experienced earlier.

"Yes, I do."

"You want to go through the tunnel of light to the other side? You want to go home?" I said, feeling the calmness slipping away again.

"No, I don't."

"Sure you do."

"No! You're a bitch!"

The calmness popped like a bubble and was gone.

"Damn right! But I'm not just a bitch, I am *the* Bitch!" I said, and laughed.

She didn't expect me to be happy about being called a bitch, and was shocked into silence for several minutes. I, in turn, was surprised at her shock, but only momentarily. Elizabeth had been reared in a time when calling someone a bitch was definitely a bad thing, and here I was taking it as a compliment.

"You're strange."

"Yes. I talk to ghosts."

She ignored that comment, still refusing to believe she was dead. But I knew I would succeed where others had failed. I'm tenacious; I rarely give up on something or someone. Some of my astral friends have let me know that I'm comparable to a bull-dog when it comes to certain issues, and this was definitely one of them.

The next morning, I went to work. Elizabeth had had time to absorb the calm feelings our home radiated, and chose to tag along with me. Probably because she really liked the attention I was paying to her.

"Is this where you work?"

"Yes."

"It's a big store," she said, her excitement growing. "Does it have clothes?"

"No, it's a do-it-yourself home-improvement store," I said, looking at the building. "I work in the hardware department."

"But you're with a man; you don't look—" She stopped.

"Butch enough to work around tools?" I asked, pausing in amusement. "I'm not homosexual, but what does it matter?"

"Uh … it doesn't," she said, sounding unsure.

It felt like this was the first time in a while that her confidence in her own opinions was shaken. Good. I knew I just had to keep pushing at this chink in her armor; I had to keep trying to get her to think in a different way. This was a beginning.

"These people look like they're from the wrong side of the tracks," she said, referring to the customers in the store.

"I guess you could say that," I said as we walked back to the break room so I could clock in. "Most of them are nice, though."

A widening of the chink; more thinking going on.

After I waited on a few customers and put merchandise up, one customer, a rather large man, came over to me.

"I need a spring for my porch swing."

"The only springs we have right now are for children's swings. I don't think they'll work."

"They might. Let me see them."

I showed the man the springs. "They're weight-rated for one hundred pounds."

"Well, I need two—that'll be two hundred pounds."

"You also need to take the weight of the swing and chains into consideration, as well as who will be using the swing," I said.

"Yeah, like you and your big, fat behind!"

I nearly laughed at Elizabeth's comment, and covered it with a cough.

"It'll mainly be my wife and me."

"Your wife's got a fat ass, too!"

Somehow I was able to maintain my composure while listening to Elizabeth make rude comments about my customer and his wife and kids. I got the feeling she was trying to get me to crack up in front of this man, to gain control of the situation. Unfortunately for her, I already had years of practice with shutting out distractions like this. I still laughed after I'd finished with the customer, though.

Most of the rest of the workday went this way: my wayward hurling insults at my customers and coworkers alike. Elizabeth found this new game of hers quite amusing, and kept it up until I got off work.

The next day, she tagged along again. This time she wasn't quite so intent upon insulting everyone around me, especially after one particular customer.

"I'm looking for the screw gun with the speed saw in it," the customer said.

I began looking around for the product, but couldn't find it right away. "Here's a screw gun," I began, and looked at the package to see if it contained the speed saw.

"That's not it!" The man grabbed the box from me and threw it on the floor, then stalked away.

I took a deep breath and counted to ten. I could feel Elizabeth's shock at the man's incredible rudeness. Picking up the screw gun, I inspected it for damage before putting it back on the shelf. At least the product was well packaged!

A few customers later, I had an encounter with another rude man.

"I need a battery for an eighteen-volt Black and Decker drill," he said, showing me the old, beat-up battery he'd brought in.

"We don't carry this battery," I said, handing it back to him.

"Why the hell not?" He demanded. "You sell the damn drill!"

"The battery design changes so often that we can't carry all the batteries; our home office decides what products we carry. I have no control over it. You could always order the battery from the company."

"That's stupid! I'm going to Lowe's!"

"Have a nice day," I said calmly, and continued straightening shelves.

"Why do you put up with these idiots?" Elizabeth asked angrily.

"It's my job. A lot of these people have stress, real or imagined, in their own lives. They feel they can take out their frustrations on floor associates in a store because we can't do anything about it—if we get rude, they complain to management and we get fired."

"Do you get paid a lot?"

"Not enough to put up with some of the customers I have to deal with," I said, chuckling.

"You should treat them the same way they treat you!"

"Why would I degrade myself by stooping to their level?"

I could feel Elizabeth thinking hard. Maybe the idea of respect for others was beginning to sink in.

The next day, Colette and Dwayne decided to work on the truck after they dropped me off at work. That summer was hot even for Kentucky; the high temperature had been above ninety degrees for several weeks in a row. In addition to the heat, humidity had been filtering into our area for a couple of days, making the uncomfortably hot weather sticky as well. Dwayne decided to take a picture of his little grease monkey sitting on the engine of the truck, her hands covered in grease. Colette was hot and sweaty, but proudly showed off her hands to the camera. When I got home that night, they were both excited over the results of the digital photograph.

"Look at this picture, Mom," Colette said.

"You've caught a wayward in it," I said, after Dwayne had pulled up the photograph on the computer.

The picture showed a rather solid fog to Colette's right, in two distinct pieces, and an orb to her left. Dwayne began playing with the enhancements, and we could make out the form of what looked like a person, reclining sideways, but in two separate pieces. It was sort of a silhouette, but definitely shaped like someone lying on her side, as if purposefully posing for the picture in a 1940s pin-up style. Elizabeth.

The orb in the picture seemed to have been moving, since it was slightly blurred on one side. Dwayne clicked the mouse more. The picture was changing with the enhancements, and a sort of face came into view on the computer screen.

"And that's Colette's spirit guide!" I said with excitement.

The next day it rained, one of those light, off-and-on rains that last all day and don't do much good for the dry, parched ground. All three of us were off work and decided to run errands in the afternoon.

"I just saw a white woman, with dark hair, floating behind us," Dwayne said calmly, glancing in the rearview mirror as we drove down a damp street.

Even though Dwayne had seen Elizabeth in the photo, we hadn't really described her to him. His description matched the way we saw her: beautiful and with a 1940s hairstyle.

A day or two later, Elizabeth finally made her choice clear.

"I want to leave."

I was unsure as to whether she wanted to leave us, or to actually go home, so I pushed the point. "The only way you're going to leave is if you go to the light," I told her.

"I know. I'm ready to go home."

"Just look for the light. You're gonna love it on the other side."

"That's what you keep telling me."

"I'm a little jealous," I told her.

"When will you join me?"

"Someday. It won't seem long. I've just got more to do here."

"I see the light."

"Go to it. It's finally your time."

I felt her go home.

"Thank you for your help."

"You're welcome."

And that was how I fulfilled my third commitment.

Afterword

When she first came to us, Elizabeth was rude, especially according to 1940s norms. She needed to learn respect for others before she was ready to go home. By being around us for a few days, she was able to learn this lesson. Just lecturing someone rarely allows for much learning to take place, but if they see something demonstrated, or experience it firsthand, it is much more effective. Without her armor of rudeness, Elizabeth was ready to accept that she needed to go home. She saw me be respectful to rude customers for hours on end during my work shifts. She saw me be respectful to polite customers as well, but she learned the most from the more difficult ones I dealt with. You always learn better from a difficult situation than from an easy one.

It's always nice when we get verification of what we're seeing and hearing. Not only did Dwayne see Elizabeth in the rearview mirror, but he also was able to capture her "image" in the digital photograph. It had been a hot, humid day and the conditions were right for seeing ghosts (and spirits) in digital media. Somehow the way that digital cameras work allows them to pick up the vibrations and/or energy of things around us that we don't necessarily see. Ghosts and spirits are pure energy, so when there's a lot of humidity in the atmosphere, they can be photographed with a digital camera more easily than with a film camera. We all know that electricity—energy—can be conducted more easily through water than air, and this is the reason that you can feel, hear, or see a ghost more easily in humid conditions than in dry ones.

Truth be told, I had been having a lot of doubts about the work I do just a few weeks before Elizabeth came to me. An experience involving an old Native man, whom a friend of mine had asked me to help, had really shaken my confidence in myself. I felt like maybe things were all in my head, maybe I was going crazy. My experience with Elizabeth did a lot to restore my belief in my work.

The incident with the old Native man was unique and, now that I understand it, proved to be a true learning experience. His first wife had been murdered years ago, and her ghost had been troubling him ever since. (It had been an arranged marriage, and neither of them had been happy.) The wife had gone alone to the white section of town to get a birthday gift for their young son, and some white men had raped and murdered her. The old Native obviously felt that if he had gone with her, she would not have been murdered.

The old man was well versed in Native spirituality and could feel his wife's ghost around him all the time. He would often complain that she caused all kinds of problems in his daily activities. Having already experienced firsthand what a cranky wayward can do to a physical person, I felt sympathy for the old man. I told my friend that I'd help.

There have been several times when I've pulled a wayward to me in order to cross it, and I seemed able to do this with the murdered Indian woman. I was anticipating a cranky ghost, so it surprised me when a rather sad one appeared before me. She was wearing a yellow dress with small blue flowers printed on it.

Again, I was rather surprised when she went home quite quickly. The next time I spoke to my friend, I told her I had been successful in crossing the old man's wife. I shared my surprise that she did not seem to be as awful as her husband had made her out to be.

But it didn't take long for my confusion about this to clear up. Soon after the wife had crossed, my friend told me that the Native man was reporting that his wife was still around him. This is what shook my faith in my work. But I should have thought more deeply about the whole situation to begin with, and used my intuition more. I did some path-walking, and discovered that the man had subconsciously created a tulpa—a thought form—of his wife, because of his guilt about allowing her to go into town alone. I had in fact crossed his wife (who really was wayward), but the tulpa continued to harass him.

The thought form he'd created had been with him so long (about three decades) that it was too powerful for me, or anyone physical whom I'm aware of, to neutralize or destroy, especially without tremendous help from its creator. But he was totally in denial that he had created this thought form; he just refused to accept the idea. Although I felt sorry for the old man, I had to let him deal with the consequences of his guilt by himself. There was nothing I could do to help him. So, reluctantly, I let go and let God.

There are several good books on tulpas or thought forms, but I strongly advise anyone who wishes to delve further into this subject to use tremendous caution. A thought form may start out innocently, but it can grow to take over the creator's life and wreak havoc all around if certain precautions are not observed. Please be aware of this.

The incident with the old Native taught me that I needed to be aware of the extenuating circumstances that can surround a haunting. Believe me, I won't make the mistake again of thinking that all hauntings are simply what they appear to be. I will definitely be more aware that there are people who are spiritually aware enough to create tulpas, whether they are conscious of them or not. And even if they are aware of their creation(s), they may not be aware enough to know what is going on around them.

Part of the old man's problem with accepting my advice was that he could not accept that a white woman could help him. He was too elitist to consider the fact that not everyone has to be born on a Native American reservation or have Native blood running through their veins to be spiritually aware—nor do you necessarily need to be Wiccan or any other specific religion. Even though my grandfather was at least one-quarter Native, I don't believe that my heritage has anything to do with my spirituality. As I stated before, the man was well versed in Native spirituality, but I have been exposed to a variety of spiritual perspectives, from different cultures and dimensions, with the help of books, path-walking, and my guides.

The whole experience with Elizabeth, however, really restored my confidence in my gut feelings and abilities. She gave me a special gift by appearing to Dwayne and "posing" for her picture with Colette that hot summer day. She gave me the gift of renewed faith—that I am doing what I committed to do, and that we really can help earthbound souls to go home.

Colette and I have been crossing waywards for years now, and are so used to it that we hardly need to give a second thought to raising our vibrations to communicate with the ghosts. It's kind of like learning how to drive. At first you really need to concentrate on putting the car into gear, or shifting with a clutch, but after a while, it becomes automatic. You don't even think about it; you just do it. The main thing we concentrate on now is what the ghost wants—and sometimes you have to use a little more edge to your argument. I used this edge with Elizabeth. She was so convinced that she was alive and healthy that I had to be a little rough with her. She didn't like me arguing with her, but I didn't like her attitude that she could stay earthbound. My desire and determination won out, and she eventually realized that she needed to go home.

Pool Hall Jenny

"You're going to like this pool hall," Dwayne said as we drove down a street in Louisville. "They serve food here, too."

"Good, I'm starving."

I knew I didn't stand a chance of winning a game against my pool-shark fiancé unless he let me win, and he knew I really didn't like it when he did that. If I was going to win, it would be by pure luck.

We saw an ambulance go around us and pull the wrong way down a one-way street. It stopped within a few yards of the corner. Another ambulance was already there, along with three police cars.

"This is a bad neighborhood. We'll leave before it starts getting dark," he said, as we saw the paramedics start to work on a person lying on the sidewalk.

I'd never been enthused about Louisville, except for the Bardstown Road and Frankfort Avenue areas, where the art galleries and cool bohemian coffee shops cater to old hippies like us, but we were in town so Colette could go to a concert by a band that she really enjoyed.

When we arrived at the pool hall, we ordered sandwiches and sodas. It was late October. We hung our jackets over the backs of the chairs and began eating as we played pool. Well … Dwayne played pool as I ate and watched. He didn't miss one shot in the first game. The next game, I tried to get one of the striped balls in a pocket, but only the solid white one would go in. The third game began much as the second did, but about halfway through it, I started sensing Jenny. Spiritual work never takes a day off.

She was a pretty African American woman, quite tall (probably around six feet), and thin but still buxom. She was every inch a woman and damn proud of it! She wore white, very fitted hot pants with a dark blue stripe down the sides and a white tank top, and had a well-kept Afro. She looked like she should be the love interest in the movie *Shaft*.

"You need to get more above the cue ball. You ain't putting enough power behind the stick."

"Okay," I said as I adjusted my stance and tuned in to how she would have hit the ball.

I actually hit the solid purple ball into the pocket! When the game was over I told Dwayne I was going out to smoke a cigarette.

"Stay in the doorway where you can see me," he said.

"No kidding!" I said as I thought about the ambulances and police cars we'd passed a few blocks away, earlier in the evening.

"This is a nasty neighborhood," Jenny said as I lit my cigarette and I looked at the parking lot of the bar across the street.

I saw two men greet each other under the street lamp and begin to talk. They didn't look too enthused with each other, and I was glad they were across the street from me.

"It doesn't look too safe." I projected my thoughts to Jenny as I watched Dwayne play pool through the open side door. "How did you come to hang out here so much?"

"I always liked playing pool," she said. "And I was good."

"I can tell."

Good, I thought to myself. *She seems to know that she's dead, but she doesn't seem to be upset by it.*

"It was hot, August, I think, and I got my sister to watch my kids while I came here. I started playing with this one dude—and I was winning—when my man came in looking for me. He was all buzzed up on heroin and started a fight with the dude I was playing with. I got in the middle. I got punched, then my man pulled a knife."

I could see only too clearly the scene as she was describing it, and felt nauseated by the amount of blood on her tank top after she'd been stabbed three times. I usually don't "see" the blood and trauma that the physical body of a ghost experienced, but her memory was so strong I couldn't help it. I tried to get her away from the memory of her own death before I lost my dinner.

"Did you see a light?"

"Yeah … I thought it was the cops, so I ran."

"Yeah, I would have run, too," I said, and paused. "You know you need to go to that light."

"Yeah … but not yet … there's just so much more I'd like to do."

I had figured that she knew she had died, at least on some level of consciousness, but by her own admission, it seemed she might be with me for a while. I didn't feel in any real hurry to cross her; her love for this world was incredibly strong, and she just needed to be reminded of how wonderful life is on the other side. She was a very enjoyable person to be around; at the same time, I knew that she needed to go home.

"You got time. You can come home with me. The light will be there when you're ready to go home."

"You know, I think I'd like that. I could hang around with a white chick for a while."

"I think I'd enjoy hanging with a black chick for a while," I said, and we both laughed.

I finished my cigarette and we went back inside. The next game, I had a lot of help from Jenny. She instructed me how to "see" the trail of the cue ball and where it would hit the ball I was aiming for. She tried to teach me some of her more difficult moves, but given my very amateur skills at pool, they were beyond me. Still, in that game I was able to get three balls into the pocket. It was a lot of fun.

We left the pool hall just as the sun was setting. A couple of our astral friends came over and helped us give Jenny a tour of the Fourth Street Live entertainment area. The bookstore was open, large and well stocked. I began looking through the New Age section first; then we went to the history section, followed by the bargain books. I tuned in to Jenny and my astral friends as they showed her how to "pick up" the spirit of the books and page through them. I'm always fascinated by what happens around me when I tune in to it!

After purchasing a bargain book on palm reading, which I'd been wanting for some time, we went to a bar that had a bowling area in it. Dwayne ordered us both a beer and we watched a baseball game while enjoying our Coronas. Jenny and the astrals bowled an "astral" game. I could feel them laughing and having a great time.

We finished our beers and went out into the cool night air in time to hear a man on a piano, who was doing a comedy routine for the patrons of a bar across the street. We listened to the routine while we window-shopped the various delicatessens around the bar.

After a few hours, we met up with Colette and listened to the last couple songs of the concert. It was a fun night for all of us. It was after midnight before we finally started home, with Jenny.

"Cool, man! I see the light," she said as we pulled into the driveway of our home. "It's beautiful!"

I watched as Jenny walked to the back of the property and through the tunnel to her real home.

Afterword

I think this story is just really neat. I so enjoyed meeting this earth-bound soul. She was one of the few who knew she was dead, at least in a way, and was rather calm about the whole situation. I did find it strange that she seemed so spiritually aware but, at the same time, had gone wayward. I don't believe she'll ever go wayward again after this.

Meeting Jenny was a relatively recent event. I have come to be quite sensitive to feeling a wayward around me, and I seem to automatically slip into a higher vibration to be able to communicate with the soul. When I first started doing this gratifying work, I had to work myself into those higher vibrations. Of course, the fact that this happened in late October helped me to sense her. The veil is thinnest in late October and early November, and then again about six months later; during these times, physical people are able to feel, hear, and see ghosts and other phenomena more easily. Also, we were quite close to the Ohio River and its humidity.

What impressed me the most about Jenny was her giving nature. She was the first earthbound soul to purposefully help *me* with something—she actively taught me about the game of pool. I got the feeling that she had been a very giving person when she was physical, and I look forward to seeing her when my time to go home comes.

The next thing I was impressed with was her love of life. She so enjoyed not only teaching me about pool, but seeing Fourth Street Live and going through the shops and bars with us and our astral friends. When I'm out in a crowd of people, I tend to block my psychic center down so I'm not overwhelmed by the emotions of the people around me. The whole time we were kicking around downtown, though, I could feel Jenny having a great time. She perused the shelves at the bookstore, watched the television and bowled while we drank a beer at the bar, and laughed at the comic playing the piano. It was wonderful feeling her joy and love of life, even if she couldn't actively participate in a physical way.

As I'm sure you've gathered from these stories, I don't know all the answers. I make mistakes; my daughter does as well. At the same time, we try to concentrate on crossing the wayward. If you can accomplish this, then you have been successful.

The Wayward and the Dragon

"**A**re we ready, ladies?" Dwayne asked as he got his coat on.

"Yeah," I said.

"I just need to put this material up," Colette said.

We were at Daniella's house. Daniella, who is Wiccan, had just opened a gift shop in the front of her home and we were helping her fill it with product. Being Wiccan and quite sensitive to psychic phenomena, Daniella knew, when she moved in, that she had a couple of ghosts in the house. We had already crossed the ones she was aware of.

Colette lugged an armful of bolts of material into the closet of an upstairs bedroom and put them on the shelf to the left of the door. When she finished arranging them, she came out of the closet and shut the door. She grabbed her coat and put it on. Suddenly, there was a loud bang—like someone had hit the closet door with his fist. No other noise came from the closet—just silence.

Colette and I were standing by the door to the bedroom, at least ten feet away from the closet, and Dwayne was beside us.

"We didn't shut a cat in the closet, did we?" Dwayne asked, as we all stared at the closed closet door.

"No," I said. "The cats are both in the other part of the house. Besides, if it was one of the cats, it would have needed a running start to slam against the door *that* hard! I don't hear any cat noises either. If a cat was in the closet it would be making noise to get out."

"Let's go," Colette said. "This is creepy."

"It's just a wayward. I wonder why we haven't felt him before now?"

"That's why I think it's creepy! I've been up here alone and I didn't feel a wayward the whole time!" Colette exclaimed as we went downstairs and out to the truck.

The next time we went up to Daniella's shop, I asked about the earthbound souls in her house to see if she had sensed the one upstairs.

"There's the big black man in the basement," she said thought-fully. "I think he was a slave."

"No, I took care of him, remember? I get the feeling he was more of a servant and he slept down there."

"Well, I saw a little old lady upstairs. She seemed to be look-ing for something, like a necklace. It was small and shiny and it would fit in her hand." Daniella demonstrated by holding out her cupped hand. "I tried to help her, but I could never find any-thing. I figured that finding her necklace would help her go to the light. I looked under the floorboards when we replaced the carpet upstairs, but there was nothing there."

"No, she's crossed as well," I said. "The wayward we heard has a masculine feel to him. He's a small man, very depressed and sad, and he's hunched over."

"I don't know," she said. "All I've ever felt were the black man and the old woman."

"I'll try to get some information on him tonight," I said.

I received no information that night, nor did I get any the next two nights. I became somewhat perplexed over the situation, but if I ask for information three nights in a row and receive none, I know that I need to figure things out for myself. I felt that this wayward would need to be approached in some entirely new way, and this made me a bit anxious and nervous about the circumstances. He had to have realized we were now aware of him, and this could cause him to demand attention from us. I didn't want him to start messing with Daniella's electricity, like Mrs. Walton had done with me years earlier. We had already heard him bang against the closet door. If angered enough, he could start throwing things around. Daniella didn't need this in her gift shop. This wayward really needed to be crossed before he became upset enough to do some damage to the physical things or people around him. Angry and/or depressed ghosts have this potential, and I didn't want my friend to be in any danger because of him. I would have to put on my thinking cap for a while with this one.

With the help of the Internet, Colette and I did some research on Daniella's house but came up with nothing. Daniella told us that the house was built in 1929 and an addition was built in the 1970s. I began really looking at the house and asking Daniella more questions. As it turned out, the ghost was staying in the original part of the house. I kept getting the feeling that it had been completed in the spring or summer of 1929, before the stock market crashed in the fall of that year.

One evening, a few days later, Colette was again upstairs sewing and I went up to join her. I was sitting on the floor while she sat in a chair using Daniella's embroidery machine. There was a lull in our conversation.

"I did it," I heard, whispered in my ear.

It was a really creepy whisper, and I got goose bumps. This was the first time in a very long time that something a wayward said or did unnerved me, and I was a bit frightened about the whole situation.

"You did what?" I asked the ghost.

"I did it."

That's when I got a vision. It was daylight—very sunny, but there was a coldness about the vision, like it was in the middle of winter—and a man and a woman were arguing. The man shoved the woman and she fell into the closet, hitting her head on a chest to the left of the door, where the shelf was now.

He looked at the still woman and pulled her off the chest. He put his hands over his face and began weeping as he knelt beside her lifeless body. Then he got a handgun and sat in the back right corner of the closet, looking at the still woman on the floor in front of him. He put the gun in his mouth and pulled the trigger.

Thankfully, the "blood" in this vision was clear. My spirit guide knows that I have a problem with seeing blood, so when it's necessary to show me something like this, the blood is there, but it's clear, not red. If I'd seen the blood as red, I probably would have fainted. There was a lot of blood, from both the man and the woman.

Now, at least, I had something to go on. The man had killed the woman in a fit of passion, then committed suicide. It had to have been sometime after the stock market crash of late October 1929. The couple must have lost all their money and were in jeopardy of losing their brand-new house as well. It had to have been remarkably difficult. When the man realized that the woman was dead, he was overcome with guilt and shot himself.

I thought that maybe automatic writing would be a potential way to get more from the man, a name maybe, but Akala, my guide, would not allow it. The ghost was just too depressed, and I was in an emotional place in my own life—I wasn't strong enough to handle my depression as well as the earthbound soul's depression.

Then another vision came to me. In it, I was holding my small crystal ball, and a miniature dragon came out of the crystal and began to befriend the man. Eventually the dragon grew rather large, and the man climbed onto the dragon's back and they flew through the tunnel of light.

I came out of the vision and told Colette about everything I'd seen. After we'd discussed it for a while, I went downstairs.

"Daniella?"

"Yes?"

"I have to leave the wayward here for a while. My guide doesn't want me to take him with me."

"That's all right."

"I figure that since you've lived with him this long, a while longer won't make much difference. I couldn't get anything from this wayward, but I know what to do to cross him."

"Whatever you need to do," she said.

About then Colette came down and we all chatted for a while before Dwayne was ready to leave. Colette went back upstairs to straighten up the room and get her coat.

"Oh my God!" she exclaimed as she came back downstairs.

"What?" Daniella and I both asked at the same time, and giggled.

"I just saw the ghost!"

"What did he look like?" I asked, excited that she would probably describe him as I saw him.

"He was short, a little shorter than me, and had those round Harry Potter glasses on. He was dressed in a white shirt, khaki-colored pants, and brown vest."

"Was the vest opened or buttoned?" I had seen him with the vest opened.

"Opened."

"That's exactly how I see him."

"He just stood there in the doorway of the bedroom and glared at me!"

"What did you do?" I asked.

"I just stood there for a minute, then said 'Excuse me' and pushed past him to get my coat!"

Daniella and I could only laugh.

The next time we went to the shop, I took my crystal ball. I could now feel the ghost quite well, having been able to tune in to his lower vibrations. He was still in the closet. I opened the closet door and sat on the floor in the middle of the bedroom with the crystal ball, as I had seen myself do in my vision. I watched as a tiny dragon, about the size of my hand, emerged from the crystal and began perusing the room.

He was iridescent, a dark emerald green with rose pink showing through in twinkles under his scales as he moved. The horns on his head and along his spine seemed to be rounded off, not pointy and sharp like I would have expected. It was almost like he was a baby. "Brilliant" could not begin to describe this creature. In order for the wayward to feel attracted to him, the dragon was deliberately giving himself a somewhat helpless and very non-threatening appearance. He gently let the man in the closet know that he was there, but did not approach him directly.

Smart, I thought. *Very smart.*

I left the crystal ball in the room when I left, so that the way-ward and the dragon could "play" together for a few weeks. Then

I went back to cross this depressed, angry ghost. All my psychic defenses were in place; I was ready for confrontation and argument in order to get him crossed.

"I love you," came a strong message through my psychic center as I walked into the bedroom.

I was a bit surprised and slightly confused. This was the first time I had been back to the shop since leaving the crystal ball and its passenger. In my absence, the dragon had obviously worked hard and long on the wayward—who had now come out of the closet.

"I love you," he said again. "Thank you for showing me the dragon."

"You're welcome. So, you're ready to go home now?" I got directly to the business at hand.

"Yes."

Taking the crystal ball out of its protective wrapping, I held it and began concentrating so that my vibrations would equal those of the earthbound soul's and the dragon's. I wanted to watch what would happen. This was going to be a special crossing and I didn't want to miss anything!

I watched as the beautiful dragon, which had been standing near the ghost and was now about the size of a large dog, grew in size until he was as big as a horse. His horns were now more like what I imagined they should be: sharp and well-defined. The horns on his head were long and graceful, curving first toward the back of his head, then slightly away at the ends. The ghost approached the dragon and stroked its scaly neck for a few moments. I felt a pang of jealousy at the wayward being able to touch the dragon when I knew I could not. Smiling, I saw the rose pink light of love emanate from both the creature and the wayward.

"It's been a long time since I felt this way," the wayward said. "I've wasted so much time here being stupid."

"Don't dwell on that, just enjoy the love," I said.

We all enjoyed the pink light for a few more minutes before the ghost gently climbed up on the dragon's shoulders, just in front of the creature's large wings. The tunnel opened. The wings unfurled.

The dragon hunched down a little as his wings rose gracefully toward the ceiling of the bedroom. The wayward and the dragon took flight, and disappeared into the tunnel of light.

Afterword

After crossing as many waywards as we have, it still amazes me that a crossing can be as out of the ordinary as this one was. Again, each crossing involves an individual person, one who was once alive and unique in his own way. We have a lot of tools in our psychic, wayward-crossing toolbox, and it's wondrously exciting to find a new one and use it to cross an earthbound soul. The crystal ball was just such a tool; it also had the added benefit of housing a dragon willing to help with a wayward.

Having had this crystal ball for about ten years, I was really in tune with it. I knew there was a dragon in it, but the dragon was always rather aloof and really didn't communicate with me much. One cannot push a dragon to communicate if the dragon is of a mind not to do so. They remind me a lot of cats, only phenomenally intelligent. When they want attention, or in this case have a job to do, they come casually by and allow you to give them the attention they desire; otherwise, keep away! This dragon had a specific purpose that he'd chosen, and I deeply respect that. He is not a "pet," but a coworker who is there to help when the need arises. I'm excited to work with this beautiful, loving creature again. I just hope I don't need to wait another ten years for it to happen!

Music Soothes the Earthbound Soul

T he crossings that I relate in this chapter are truly special to me. Not only did I get to hear some good music, performed by talented people, but I was blessed to witness how good music can heal and comfort the soul.

The Schoolteacher

"Do you have a 'friend' around?" Dwayne asked me one day, after dropping a fork for the third time that morning.

"A wayward or an astral friend?" I asked, knowing immediately he was not talking about someone physical because we were alone in the house.

"Either one."

I stopped writing and opened myself up to whomever might be around us.

"There are a few astrals here now. Why?"

"For about three weeks now, I've been dropping things on a regular basis."

"Me too," I said, and thought for a moment. "The rummage sale where you bought that washing machine—do you know if an old lady owned it?"

A few months before, our old washing machine had died on us and Dwayne eventually found a newer one at a local church rummage sale.

"No, it was a young couple."

"Did they buy it used from an old lady?" I asked.

"No, they said they bought it about six years ago, brand new, from the Home Depot when it first opened."

"I've been feeling an old woman around ever since you brought that washer home," I insisted.

"Well, the young couple said they bought it brand new."

I began to think more deeply about the washer. Why did I feel that an old woman wayward was connected to it?

When my now ex-husband and I had first moved out to the country, we came into town occasionally and had seen the land, where the Home Depot is now located, being cleared and the building being built. I remembered feeling sad that all those beautiful trees were cut down and burned and hauled away. A vague memory of a small white house came to my mind.

"Was there a house on the land where the Home Depot was built?" I asked, knowing that Dwayne had lived in the area for almost fifteen years and might remember.

"I don't think so," he said.

"Are you sure?"

"I really don't remember if there was or not," he said after putting a little thought into the question.

A few days later, I was in the break room at work having lunch and chatting with one of our assistant store managers when the vision of the white house came into my mind.

"Hey, Richard," I started, knowing that he'd lived in town for a number of years. "Before Home Depot was built, was there a small white house on the property?"

"I think there was," he said, after thinking about it.

"Over toward the mall," I stated.

"I believe you're right."

"Do you know who lived there?"

"I think it was abandoned."

That had to be it. There must have been an old woman living in that house sometime before it was torn down. Why she was attached to the washing machine would be anyone's guess.

That night I tried to make contact with the quiet old woman, but she refused all my attempts. The next several days produced the same results. But I wasn't worried. The only thing she seemed to be affecting was our grip on things; dishes and other objects would periodically fall from our grasp.

That Saturday, we went to Lexington to a bohemian coffee shop near the University of Kentucky. Anna, our musician friend, had invited Dwayne to play bongos and the djembe on stage with her. Mark, her husband, had picked us up so we could carpool.

Thinking about the old lady wayward was the furthest thing from my mind at that time, but after Dwayne and Anna, with another of Anna's friends on back-up guitar, began to play, I started to sense her in the café with us.

Anna is a schoolteacher, and introduced one of her songs by explaining that it was about a child who was a composite of some of the children in her classes. I felt the earthbound old woman become quite interested as the ballad began.

This time, when I began to talk to her, she actually answered.

149

"So, you like my friend's music?" I asked, relieved that she was finally showing interest in something other than the washing machine, for the first time in the month she'd been with us.

"Yes, it's very soothing. It's not like what I usually hear."

"Yeah. She sings really well."

"I used to be a schoolteacher. This song is very true."

We listened to the song, and the next. The song after that was about Anna's grandmother, Beatrice, and how she had loved life and lovingly teased her friends and family.

"You know . . . you could meet Beatrice and teach school again."

"Really?" the old woman asked, her attention piqued.

"Sure, on the other side of the light."

"I saw a light once. It seems so long ago."

"You can see it again and go to the other side. You'll really like it there. It's beautiful on the other side of the light."

"I'm sure it is."

I felt the tunnel of light begin to form. Calmness and that familiar nausea swept over me.

"You should go to the light. Your family and friends are waiting for you."

"Gertrude," she said as she went into the tunnel.

After the concert, Colette and I went out to the patio to smoke a cigarette; Anna and Mark joined us. Mark and I were talking about the "ghosty" book I was in the process of writing.

"We had an old lady wayward attached to the washer we just got a few weeks ago, and I crossed her tonight," I told Mark, as Anna sat down next to me.

"Really?" Anna said. "That's kind of creepy."

"Why? Because she hitched a ride with us to Lexington?"

"Yeah . . . and that she was out in the audience the whole time."

"Well, maybe not the whole time," I said. "She liked the song about your student—she was a schoolteacher, too—and she left

150

after the song about your grandmother. She said 'Gertrude' before she left. I think that was her name."

"It's just a little creepy," Anna repeated, laughing nervously.

The Wayward and the Angels

A few weeks after that, we were invited out to Mark and Anna's house for a free concert they were throwing to record her songs into an album.

They live in an old farmhouse by Rough River, which they'd been fixing up since they moved in. The house is over a century old. During the previous summer, Dwayne had laid floors in their living room, hallway, and kitchen, with a little help from me. We'd torn up the old pine flooring in the general store in front of the house, cleaned and sanded the boards, and put them back down the old-fashioned way, with hammer and twist flooring nails. In the hallway, Dwayne, an accomplished artist, made a thunderbird out of the wood planks. One of the planks had a rather large knot in it, which he used as the bird's eye. The look was somewhat subtle, but beautiful. He then used his wood-burner to add tribal art to some of the smaller planks along the wall, around the thunderbird.

Whenever I was there to help with the floor, I'd felt a darkness about the house. I would cross a dark wayward or two, every time. But this summer, I felt no dark ones as I roamed around their forty acres of land. It seemed quite peaceful.

"We had my parents over here a couple of weeks ago," Mark said, sitting down across from me at the dining room table, where I was writing.

"Did y'all have a nice visit?" I asked, turning my attention to him.

"It was interesting," he said and paused, thinking about the visit from their out-of-town guests. "You know, we show off the floors to everyone who comes over. We're quite proud of them."

"Why, thank you. They turned out beautifully. I truly believe that there's nothing that Dwayne can't do."

"Yeah. They first saw the floors when they visited right after you'd finished it, and of course were very impressed."

"Of course," I said, and grinned.

"Well, my parents asked if we'd done anything else to the house since you all had done the floor. We said 'no,' of course, because we haven't. Then they asked if we had done any major cleaning. No, just the regular stuff. Then they said that the house felt cleaner … lighter."

"Cool," I said, smiling and knowing that his parents had felt the lightness of the atmosphere in an unhaunted house. Then Mark dropped the bomb.

"So I told them about you and what you do," he said in the same steady voice, watching for my reaction. He got it.

"What?" I asked. My calmness and joy about what he was telling me shattered.

I rarely talk about my wayward wrangling, and when I do, it's usually with someone I've known for a while or someone who brings up the subject of ghosts. If I don't know the person well, I speak in vague terms so as not to frighten them. For the most part, I get the feeling that people don't believe that Colette and I do what we do and they think we're crazy. So be it. So, I had never expected Mark to say anything to anyone about what I'd done to clear out the dark ones from their property. When I'd first told him and Anna about it, in fact, they'd looked at me like they could see that third horn growing out of my head. I'd decided that I just would not mention it again unless they did … and of course, Mark eventually asked me more questions and got pretty much the whole story from me. He truly seemed fascinated by what Colette and I do.

"Yeah," Mark continued, when I wasn't able to say anything else. "I don't think they believed me, but they couldn't deny that the house felt better to them."

"Well, that's good." I smiled.

It's always nice to get confirmation that what we're doing works, especially from people who don't necessarily believe in what we do.

Later that evening, as the sun set, the concert began. As I was enjoying the music, however, I began to sense something rather ominous.

The makeshift stage was on an old concrete slab that might have once been part of a smokehouse or some sort of storage house. It was butted up against a heavily forested hill, where large rocks bounced the music back to the audience. It was the perfect set-up for a performance.

Dwayne was in the back, stage left, with one of the huge boulders directly behind him. In the darkness of that small alcove I could feel a large African American man sitting behind him. He didn't really seem to be enjoying the concert much. His attention seemed to be focused on me, and I was a little unnerved by it.

Dwayne was again playing the bongos and the djembe, but this time he added the xylophone's voice to the music. Somehow I was able to hear the music in the way that the big earthbound soul was hearing it. It was kind of a strange stereo sound in my head, and when Dwayne tapped the xylophone it sounded dull and clunky, instead of making the beautiful notes I'd been hearing.

"Do you not like the bell sound?" I asked the ghost.

There was no response.

"When I'm on the other side I play bells. My favorite song to play is 'Carol of the Bells.' It's the only Christmas song I will never tire of," I said, thinking ahead to another retail Christmas and the same forty or so Christmas songs played on the P.A. system, over and over, during the four weeks between Thanksgiving and Christmas.

Again, there was no response, even after I tried to send him a picture of what I remembered of the other side and the beautiful music there.

I left the big, uncommunicative wayward alone after that.

After the concert we went home, and I didn't think much more about the wayward. He didn't seem to be interested in going into the house, so I wasn't worried about him disturbing Mark and Anna. Mark had mentioned to me, several months before, that the farm once had servants on it, so I figured the next time I went to their house I would try to cross this earthbound soul, who probably had been a servant.

Less than a week later, the Kentucky State Fair opened and P.O.D. was giving a free concert, with Pop Evil as the opening act.

After a couple or three of Pop Evil's songs, I felt the big wayward behind and to the left me. I figured that he must have followed me home, because we had not been back to Mark and Anna's house since the concert. I could feel his anger pouring over me.

"How do you like the concert?" I asked.

"I don't want to be here." His voice was an extremely low rumble in my head.

"You know, these guys are pretty good. Listen to what they're saying in their songs. See their energy."

The big man was quiet for a while as we listened to the new band.

"All right," he rumbled.

About that time, I noticed angels appearing on the roof of Cardinal Stadium, their wings held slightly away from their bodies.

"Do you see the angels?" I asked.

There was no comment.

"They're dancing to the music," I said, as I watched them bounce and sway to the beat.

There was a low grunt this time.

Pop Evil finished their set and P.O.D. was announced. The crowd roared and jumped up, waving and clapping with deafening excitement.

"And now—P.O.D.," the man from the radio station said. "Payable On Death!"

I felt shock from the ghost behind me. He knew his physical body was dead. I tensed a little; this could get tricky. I knew I had to keep my head and focus on him. At the same time, I didn't want to miss any of the show, so I split my attention between the wayward and P.O.D. (a difficult thing to do when one of your favorite bands is singing for you).

Usually, when a wayward knows his physical body is dead, he has a bad attitude toward everything. This bad attitude can be directed toward people, or he can choose to manipulate the energy around him. Either way, physical people can be harmed. There was a lot of energy at this concert, both from the electricity for the lights and stage equipment and from the band and the audience. In addition, the sun had set and the cooling temperature meant the Ohio River's humidity was getting more pronounced. The atmosphere was ripe for the manipulation of energy.

About then I remembered the angels. There was a particularly large one behind the big wayward, as well as several others around us. I relaxed to the soothing calmness that was radiating from God's helpers. Divine help is always given when it is needed, and I was awed and thankful for it. I knew the ghost would cross, and I knew what song would be the crossing song.

"Youth of the Nation" began, and Dwayne, Colette, and I sang along with most of the rest of the audience. By now I could feel the big earthbound soul begin to relax. He really seemed to be enjoying the performance of the band and the presence of the angels. Several songs later, the band played "Alive" as their final song.

155

"You know you need to go to the light," I said, remembering the video of the song and projecting it to the wayward as it played in my head.

"Yes. I'm ready."

"You can wait until they finish the song."

"I would like that."

His voice was still a low rumble, but it seemed much clearer to me. I was definitely better able to understand what he was saying.

Again, all were singing, and the tunnel began to form just beyond the stage, to my far right.

"It's beautiful," the big wayward said.

"Yes, it is," I said as the nausea washed over me.

The angels began to gather around the tunnel and along the path to it. It truly was a beautiful sight. The song ended and the crowd roared with ecstasy. Indescribably beautiful music filled my head—homecoming music. The big earthbound soul got up from his seat and began walking to the light. As he passed the angels, they fell in step behind him. It was like he was leading them back to heaven and God's waiting arms.

Afterword

Dwayne makes and plays wooden Cherokee love flutes. When he plays a concert on stage and I take pictures with our digital camera, the pictures almost always have orbs around him. Once, when I took pictures of him playing at a Louisville bar for open mic night, one photo in particular had so many orbs in it that it looked like Dwayne had a bubble machine on stage with him! It's really neat when spirits from the other side, as well as earthbound souls, sit in on a concert.

In the two stories in this chapter, music helped the waywards realize that they needed to cross over and go back home. This was not the only time that music has played a role, of course; the first time was when we played Queen and John Denver for Marie in

Our Pet Wayward. The difference in these instances was that the music was performed live instead of played on a CD. Live music is infinitely more enjoyable!

The old lady who was attached to the washing machine had seemed very depressed to me. This is probably why I didn't feel her right away (it was the same with the man in *The Wayward and the Dragon*). She had probably lived by herself for so long before her physical body died that she just didn't talk much. That's all right, though; she liked the song our friend was singing and eventually crossed.

When it came to the African American wayward, I have a feeling that in life he tended to stay away from white folks as much as he could. Dwayne may have helped him feel more comfortable because of his dark-colored skin, and that's why the ghost sat behind him at the concert at the farmhouse.

The video of the song that this earthbound soul crossed to, P.O.D.'s "Alive," shows a car wreck; the driver survives and is filled with joy at this. I feel that most of the adults in the audience had seen the video and were picturing it as the song was performed. I really think this had a lot to do with the big wayward crossing. There was also so much loving energy coming from the audience—the ghost didn't stand a ghost of a chance of not crossing!

This was another one of those crossings where divine help was needed (although I was unaware I needed it, at first) and given. I will remember this crossing for a long time to come.

Part Two

the waywards
& you

How to Cross a Wayward

I hope that by reading the stories in the first part of this book, you have been able to gain an understanding of waywards. I tried to write about earthbound souls who were noticeably different from each other—some are serious, some are angry, some are polite, and some are funny. Together, they illustrate how a person's soul and personality can survive physical death. Yet with all waywards, no matter how unique, the key is to approach them as individuals ... to treat them with respect and love, holding out your hand to help them.

Of course, the first thing to remember if you encounter a wayward in your own life is to not be afraid! Primarily, a wayward just wants to go home, to where there's peace and love. It's that simple. What can be challenging is giving the ghost the second-ary reason it wants to go home, so that it will use free-will choice to get there. Getting the ghost to choose to go to the light is a lot easier and less traumatic than forcing it, as we have to do with the dark entities. The earthbound soul learns that the light is a good thing, and when it's time to cross again, after its next life, it will go home instead of becoming wayward again.

But as you have read, it can get tricky when the wayward is waiting for something or someone. Marcella, at the end of the *Commitments* story, was waiting for her house to be renovated. When I finally convinced her that her house was complete, she crossed over. The majority of the Confederate solders in *The Men in Gray* were waiting for their orders. The earthbound soul always wants to cross; it's just a matter of remembering that that's what it truly wants to do. Overall, once you figure out what the way-ward wants, you can provide it.

Just don't lie, which will cause problems the next time the soul tries to cross. For example, if an earthbound soul wants to know if a specific person is on the other side, don't say yes unless you are *absolutely positive* the other person is there *and* that the earthbound soul will be happy about it. Colette and I just say there's someone on the other side who can explain who is there and who is not. Always be safe when it comes to gaining an earth-bound soul's trust. Fortunately, most waywards want something, as opposed to someone.

Sometimes the things you might have to say can sound extreme, even if they are truthful. The results are what matter. Once, in an episode I didn't include in this book, Colette and I argued a way-ward over by telling him he could better help us find his killer if he was on the other side. This was true, but once the wayward crossed, he was no longer worried about physical justice because he knew that there would be divine justice in time. Time on the other side is nothing like it is here in the physical world; a short time at home could mean years of linear earthly time. And it's up to God whether or not there will be physical justice, where an offender is punished for a specific crime in the physical world, or a spiritual reckoning, where the offender is made to see his offense after he's crossed. Or both. Just remember not to judge another soul; that job is just way too big for us!

Much of the time, when a soul goes wayward, it's because the death of the physical body was sudden and unexpected. But sometimes in these cases, the soul just needs to linger a short time to learn something from the circumstances surrounding its death. For example, there was a woman in our town who died in a car wreck. Dwayne was taking me to work one rainy day in mid-December; we had gotten a late start, and were about a mile away from my workplace when traffic slowed to a stop. We eventually saw the wreck, which took over two hours to clear away. We were lucky that we had not been involved, since it was directly in our path.

The woman in the accident died later that night, and Colette and I tuned in to her troubled spirit. She was confused and upset; so were we. Colette and I were feeling guilty over being glad about Dwayne and I surviving when someone had died. But we didn't try to cross the woman. Her soul may have had something to learn from what happened in the physical world because of her death. And in fact, on the day of her funeral, the woman crossed on her own. We'd been hoping this would happen. So keep an eye out whenever you are aware of a quick, traumatic, or unexpected death, and remember that a wayward might just need a little time. But if the soul stays wayward, or seems lost or stuck, try to get it crossed as quickly as possible.

If crossing waywards is your calling, you will soon be able to feel, see, or hear ghosts on a regular basis. Not everyone who dies will go wayward, but enough people do that this skill is well worth honing.

A Guide to Meditation

In order to be able to communicate with wayward spirits, you need to be sensitive to higher vibrations. You have to be able to psychically tune in to their presence. If you've lost this ability in your adult years, you can get it back. Prayer is one way to accomplish this. Prayer is just talking to God. Colette and I also do a lot of meditating. Meditation is just listening to God—calming your mind, raising your vibrations to a higher level, and connecting with your higher self. When the higher self has a pathway to the conscious self, you're more psychically in tune with your surroundings.

The more you do this kind of work, the easier it will be to make these connections and sense the ghost who needs crossing.

Sit in a comfortable chair and relax. Your feet should be flat on the floor and your arms should be resting on the armrests of the chair or on your thighs. The idea is to be as comfortable as you can without going to sleep! The first thing you will want to do is to set up a protective barrier around yourself before you get too far into your meditation.

Think of a beautiful, pure white light centering in your solar plexus, the area of your stomach that your rib cage partially encloses, just below the end of the breastbone. This is your diaphragm. Push this light out around your physical body and tell it to protect you for the rest of this incarnation, to always be around you and to grow in strength as you grow in wisdom and learn from this lifetime. This psychic shield will protect you in ways that you cannot imagine. Once the shield is up, *never* take it down. You can also push another shield, in the same manner, out around your car, house, whatever, and the dark ones will not be able to come through it. To keep the shields around inanimate objects strong, you'll want to program them to take necessary energy from the elements around them. Also tell the shield to "split for unawares," as we put it; that way, physical people can come and go through the shield and not damage it.

Meditation is a calming of your mind, so try to think only of the task at hand: crossing the wayward and possibly communicating with it. Relaxing enough to do this may take a few minutes, but it can be done. Some people think of a bright (but not unbearable) white light, between and just above their eyes. This is the third eye, where the gift of psychic sight is located in the physical body.

If other thoughts distract you while you're meditating, like what you'll be fixing for dinner or what the weather is like, think of them briefly, then gently push them from your mind to return to at a later time. Don't get frustrated; just let the thoughts slip away and get back to the task at hand.

Meditation like this will open you up to communication from the other side. The spirits who have crossed over want us to succeed at what we do, and are willing to help in any way they can. If we calm our minds enough, their communication can be heard, seen, or felt. You might hear an actual voice or maybe a sound, even a bit of a song, which would be a clue as to what the ghost needs in order to cross. You could see a vision, or a clip from a movie or television show that would help. Or you could feel a touch or change in temperature. Some of these clues will be symbolic. This is where you will need to think about what the symbolism means to you (or to the wayward), specifically.

While in a meditative state, ask God (or whatever higher power you believe in) to help you be successful in crossing the wayward(s) and guiding them to the light. Sometimes you may get a vision or a flash of inspiration. If this happens, go with it and use it to your advantage. This will be a message from either your higher self or from the spirit world. That's what happened for me in *The Men in Gray* story. Grounding helped get me into a calm mindset, where I could open my third eye to what was going on around me.

But don't be upset if you don't get any "messages." Sometimes desire and determination alone will give you what you need to push the earthbound soul to the other side, as was the case for us in *Our Pet Wayward*. What I'm trying to say is, go with the flow, allow the wayward to give you clues as to what to do, and improvise.

Your ability to meditate will improve if you do it on a regular basis. I meditate before I go to sleep at night. This helps me calm down from an exciting or frustrating day and allows sleep to come more quickly. After years of doing this, I can slip into a meditative state within a few minutes, even if I have a lot on my mind. There are even times now that I can meditate while standing up or doing a simple or boring task, like washing dishes or doing the laundry. What I'm trying to say is that after a while, you will be able to slip into a calm, controlled state quickly and sometimes without much effort, no matter what distractions are on your mind or around you physically. You just have to meditate consistently to achieve this goal.

If you want to learn more about meditation, there are several good books out there that go into more detail and illustrate other methods (also, see the Suggested Reading at the back of this book). Find the method that works best for you and use it. I can't tell you what the right method is for you personally, just what works best for me.

Intuition Meets Determination

The process of meditation allows you to open up to your intuition, as well. As a rule, Colette and I use intuition when it comes to crossing waywards. In other words, we sense what the wayward wants. Most of the time we go into a haunting cold, without prior knowledge, as in *The Walmart Waywards* and *The Men in Gray*, and…well…as in most of the other stories in this book. We don't always know there is a ghost around before we sense it. After years of experience, though, we've gotten to where we can tell if an area, house, or place is haunted. We do get visions and clues from the other side during these times. We usually let the wayward lead us in the direction we need to go to get it crossed. Most of the time, waywards are quite communicative in this respect; they just want to talk to someone, to have their loneliness relieved.

Basically, a ghost is a person without a physical body—just the soul or essence of the person. Most of them have a need to be social with other people. Physical people, if the wayward can sense them (much in the way we sense the wayward), tend to just "ignore" ghosts. And most people, whether physical or not, don't like to be ignored! So when someone senses an earthbound soul and starts communicating with it, the earthbound soul is usually grateful.

You can also learn a lot about waywards from your dreams. Most of the time these dreams are pretty straightforward, as was my dream of drawing the circles in *Candi's Mother-in-Law*. Occasionally they are symbolic (there was some symbolism in the dream I had about Nimbi in the *Commitments* story, but there was a lot of symbolism in the dream I had about the young girl, the dream I later realized was about my commitments). These dreams can help you figure out what the ghost wants and/or how to cross it. Then do your best to convince the earthbound soul, as quickly as possible, to cross. The time that a soul is wayward is wasted time when it could be learning lessons and perfecting itself for God. But it is interesting that the first (and so far only) time a ghost ever admitted this to me was in *The Wayward and the Dragon*.

God wants us all to come back home. Mom and Dad love us and only want the best for us, but they are not going to interfere with our learning processes. We are given the means and desire to learn; what we do with these tools is our own free-will choice. Some of us choose to be stupid and ignore these wonderful and useful tools. We allow them to sit out in the rain and rust, but we can bring them back in and clean them up and use them for our betterment, as well as for the good of those around us.

Colette and I do not charge money for our services. For the most part, we have crossed earthbound souls without anyone knowing we've done so. This, to us, just prevents a lot of hassle. We have occasionally accepted gifts or a meal, but never money. We feel that personal gain from our gifts would compromise them; we would lose them if we accepted money for doing God's work. God gives us abilities out of the love, and we should use them in the same way. We still have to live, of course, so we keep regular jobs for this purpose. Spiritual work is spiritual, and you should love and have a love of spiritual work if you want to cross waywards.

Then again, love is the reason we are all here. If you do not love … if you have fear in your heart … it will be difficult, if not impossible, to cross waywards. After dealing with Mrs. Walton, I have not felt fear (except for the occasional twinge) when it comes to ghosts. Occasionally I've felt fear about not being able to cross a ghost, but it's been a long time since I've felt even that kind of fear. And as I've mentioned, desire and determination are big factors in this line of work. Yes, there have been a few times when I didn't want to deal with a cranky or stubborn wayward (as in *Who Fed Socrates Cheez-Its?*), but those times have been few and far between. We are all human and imperfect. If we were perfect, we would be God, not souls on this dark rock learning hard lessons about love. The goal is that the waywards get crossed, one way or another.

Resources

If you are interested in ghost stories, you've realized by now that most of the books, shows, or movies about ghosts are only about the haunting part—the drama of the situation. The authors of these books and shows don't try to cross the souls or help them find the peace they need. Maybe they just don't know how to accomplish this task. I hope my book can help change that. The book that inspired me, *Phantoms Afoot* by Mary Summer Rain, is similar to the one you are reading now, but the author tends to be vague about how she actually crosses the waywards. I didn't benefit from this approach. I'm sure that some of the things she learned from her mentor are better kept "secret" because of their origin, but at the same time, I really wanted to know how to cross waywards so I could help these lost souls as well. My desire and determination, as well as a lot of inner path-walking, gave me the knowledge to be able to do this rewarding volunteer work. Now I'm sharing it with you.

Another good book, although it doesn't deal specifically with crossing earthbound souls, is *Speaking with the Dead* by Konstantinos. Konstantinos shares some very valid spiritual truths that could help in your quest to learn more about this wonderful line of volunteer work. This book mostly focuses on speaking with spirits (those who have successfully crossed over), but the methods in it could easily be used to communicate with earthbound souls as well. If you'd like to use some of the methods in his book, please do; just get the wayward crossed afterward! Remember to avoid the temptation to keep a wayward as a pet. While I don't approve of this approach, in my work I respect the boundaries that unenlightened individuals have set up. If people know they have a ghost and don't want me to cross it, I do not force the issue. I know that eventually, the wayward will find its way back home.

Not everyone who reads this book, of course, will want to learn to cross waywards with the intensity and dedication that Colette and I do. Not many people, understandably, are cut out for this kind of work! But if you feel this way, don't look upon it as a failure. The thing that matters is your willingness to help a wayward cross, if and when a ghost comes to you and you have the means to help it. And always remember, any fear you may feel about this work is much worse than the work itself! The act of helping a ghost go home is very rewarding, as we hope you've seen through the stories in this book. If you have the potential to help, or know of someone who could cross a wayward you've encountered, what's the big deal? Just do it.

The waywards Colette and I have helped go home are grateful to us. I suspect that when it is our time to go home, a lot of them will be waiting for us on the other side of that tunnel of light. We'll be having one big party when we reach the other side—I can hardly wait!

How to Find Waywards

If you do feel ready to commit to this work, or at least ready to explore it further, you may be wondering where the waywards are, exactly. Finding waywards is different for different people. For example, for some time now Colette and I have considered ourselves ghost magnets. Waywards find us, and neither of us are really sure how or why. But everyone, physical and nonphysical alike, has at least a little bit of intuition, and we think that's how the majority of earthbound souls find us. They sense that we can help them, even if they don't even consciously realize it.

So, just projecting your willingness to help can be one way to draw waywards to you. For example, one day after we'd moved from our house in the country to a place in town, our dog Madison started barking at a ghost who'd wandered in. He was a big man who was mentally handicapped. He ran away from Madison but got stuck at the boundary of our shield, which we'd modified to keep earthbound souls from leaving once they got through it. (They can come in through the shield, but can't leave unless they go to the light.) Colette went outside, gently calmed him down, and told him to go to the light—which the wayward did right away. He'd been drawn to us because we could tell him that.

Waywards may appear to you in your dreams, of course, or through communications from the other side. I've found that I usually end up waiting until I meet these individuals. For example, I dreamed about a friend of mine a few weeks after her father had died. In my dream, I was in Sarah's new house in Richmond, Kentucky, where I'd never been before, and an old woman wayward was there with Sarah's father. The old woman in my dream was cranky and didn't want anyone in "her" home.

Later, I called Sarah and described the inside of her new house down to the air intake vent behind the front door. This didn't surprise her, because we've been friends for years and she accepts me having these insights. She did mention that the oxygen machine her father had used while he was alive kept having unexplained electrical problems. Ghosts have an easy time manipulating electrical currents; as pure energy, they have no physical body to interfere in this process. So this just confirmed to me that the ghost of the old woman was cranky and manipulating the energy around her. I would have to be on my toes when dealing with her. But I kept this feeling from my friend. She had young children and I didn't want to frighten her, possibly making the situation worse.

Sarah said that we were more than welcome to come over and cross her ghost. I didn't tell her that her father hadn't crossed either, because I didn't want to worry her. She loved her father very much and had taken care of him both while he was alive and while he was dying.

When Colette and I arrived at Sarah's house, we immediately felt the wayward's presence and began to work on her. We eventually had to "push" her to the other side with our desire to have her gone. When the tunnel opened up, Sarah's father crossed as well, with just a little prodding from us.

I did eventually tell Sarah that her father had gone wayward, and that we'd crossed him along with the cranky old woman ghost.

You can also find waywards by going places they would logically be. Colette and I sometimes seek out waywards—we go to a reputed haunted place after we read about it or someone tells us about it. This was the case with a couple of places in Lexington and Bardstown. The Bardstown experience was interesting. There was an earthbound soul at an old tavern who had actually been caught in a photograph. When I had an opportunity to go to the tavern, I found that she didn't like the music of the band we'd gone to listen to—she said the music was too loud. Actually, the music was always too loud and raucous for her. It took a while, and a lot of concentration on my part (with the energy from the band and patrons of the bar somewhat interfering), but I eventually convinced her that the music on the other side of the light was much better. I tuned in to what I was hearing from the other side and projected it to her (no offense to musicians still living in the physical world).

Also, someone may tell you about a ghost or ghosts that they're aware of. This was the case for us with Nimbi, in the *Commitments* story. We also encountered an earthbound soul this way in Elizabethtown, Kentucky. Colette was dating a young man whose grandparents were celebrating their fiftieth wedding anniversary at a local landmark. Colette saw a shadow move under a door that was locked, and her date confirmed that the building was rumored to have a ghost. Colette knew that no one physical was in the locked room. Her date stood guard as she quietly crossed the wayward.

You also might learn of a friend's relative, or a friend, who seems to have gone wayward. Through your connection to your friend, you can draw the earthbound soul to you. How Colette and I manage to do this is still somewhat of a mystery to us. We just know that our connection to the physical friend and our desire and determination to cross the wayward have a lot to do with it. After we draw the earthbound soul to us, we begin the work of crossing it. This was the situation when my friend Faith told me that her aunt had died. As she was telling me about her aunt, I concentrated on the aunt and Faith, and was able to pull the aunt to me and cross her over. (You may be lucky enough to have others tune in to what you're doing as well, as we did in the stories *Candi's Mother-in-Law* and *Elizabeth*.)

Keep in mind that not all the feelings you have or the noises you hear are psychic in nature. One night, when Colette and I were alone after Dwayne had left for work, our dogs started barking and running to the door several times. After we looked out and saw no one there, we noticed that the noise that had set off the dogs was our storm door, blowing open and shut in the wind. Along these lines, the rustling you hear in the tall grass when you're walking by an old abandoned house is most likely just a small animal or bird, not a wayward. On a cold day, the wisp of fog you see around your house could be due to the fact that you're drying clothes and steam is escaping from the dryer vent.

But sometimes, you'll hear or see something that has no physical explanation. In *Our Pet Wayward*, Marie jiggled the gate to the fence around our front yard. And when I heard what I thought were the garbage cans banging against the house that windy night, I found the cans secure against the wall and not flying around the yard as I'd expected—so I knew it was a psychic sound. What I'm trying to say here is that if you experience some-thing unusual, investigate it. If there's no physical reason for it, then there's a psychic reason. The rule of thumb is to investigate first, and see if there's an explanation for what you hear or see.

Ghosts are real. As you have seen in this book, the methods Colette and I use are not always conventional, but success is always achieved. As you can tell, crossing waywards can take time—days or even weeks. Sometimes there's a lot of work and research involved. Research is a good thing, and we try to do at least some when we have time and the access to research facilities. (This usu-ally happens when we need to learn something peripheral about the ghost or the situation that it's in.) Sometimes the research is fruitful, as it was with Mrs. Walton in *The Haunted House on Main Street*. Sometimes it's not, as in *Our Pet Wayward* and *The Wayward and the Dragon*. But in both of these instances, we still learned something that had to do with the earthbound soul we were deal-ing with. Most of the time, Colette and I fly by the seat of our pants and go with our intuition, knowing that we're trying our best and, even though it may take time, we will succeed in getting the earthbound soul back home.

Despite all the resistance I felt when I first became aware of my commitments, I really love helping out lost souls. It's the most satisfying, gratifying volunteer work I can imagine, and I'm so glad to have it as my second job. Or is it my primary job? If you start working in this field, you just might feel the same way.

A Note on Dark Waywards

I cannot conclude this book without a caution regarding dark waywards. They are the most dangerous kind of ghost, and only the experienced should tackle them. Dark waywards are those who have gone completely to the wrong side of the good/ evil equation. They have no redeeming qualities whatsoever, as far as physical people are concerned. Their redemption lies in going home, to the only ones who can help them: Mom and Dad. There is so much fear in their souls that there is no room for love at all. They fear everything, and that fear makes them spiteful, resentful, cruel—any negative emotion you can think of. Just like when they existed in the physical world.

When someone allows fear to take over and control life, he or she can turn dark very easily. As Master Yoda said in the *Star Wars* movies, "Fear is the path to the dark side." Basically, fear is the opposite of love. When you fill your heart and life with love ... when you allow the light of love into your heart ... darkness flees. Love can create miracles. Love can lift a car off a loved one. Love can accomplish goals only dreamed of. With love, "all things are possible." Love is a giving of yourself without expecting anything in return. This giving of yourself, without desire for reward, is what creates the energy that can help you create miracles.

I have run across a few dark waywards in my time. One of them is described in *The Men in Gray*. That dark soul was quite dangerous, and could affect physical things around him. Another time, a young man Colette was dating told us about an eerie feeling he had while visiting a local lake. When we went to the lake, we initially went to the opposite side; there, we found a dark ghost. He charged at me. My shield, which I'd programmed to protect myself, reached out and grabbed him. It happened so quickly that I didn't have time to think. Thank goodness my shield defended me! I then concentrated on pushing my shield up, with the dark wayward in it, high above the trees. I watched as the angels swooped down and grabbed him, taking him back to the other side. In times like these, take off your kid gloves and do whatever you need to do to protect yourself and others.

Interestingly, the eerie feeling that Colette's friend had felt, on the other side of the lake, actually came from a group of earth spirits. They guarded a patch of wilderness from those who might damage it. Since Colette's friend wore glasses, the earth spirits had not been able to see his soul (and good intentions) through the lenses, and therefore made him feel uneasy and fearful, successfully chasing him away from their territory. When I finally did go to the correct side of the lake, I took my glasses off. The old one of the group saw that I was not there to do any harm, and welcomed me.

There are other waywards who can affect the physical world, but they have a different feel than the dark ones. The first wayward I helped to cross, Mrs. Walton, was as cranky as they get. She moved things around, affected electricity, and in general made me miserable. She fed off the fear and anger she created within us, but she was not dark. Mrs. Walton was what I would call "gray."

Gray waywards are fence sitters—they can go either light or dark. (Gray ones exist as people in the physical world, too, as do dark ones.) You can never know what to expect from gray waywards, so be aware. They may be nice one minute and very cruel the next. They lure you in with compliments, assurances of love, promises, half-truths, or whatever they think you want to hear, in order to gain control over you. I'm sure we all know someone physical like this. Colette and I have run across several gray waywards in our work; for example, the woman who wanted to kill her husband again (she was dark gray), Candi's mother-in-law, and the man in *The Wayward and the Dragon*.

Gray ghosts and dark ghosts are not to be confused with earthbound souls who have righteous anger. The wayward in the ravine in *The Men in Gray* was neither gray nor dark; he just had a tremendous amount of anger about being murdered … and rightly so.

As you've seen in the stories, all the gray waywards we've encountered have been crossed. Sometimes it takes time, but gray ones can be convinced to go to the light by showing them logic or the error of their ways. Dark waywards, however, won't listen to this kind of reasoning; Colette and I don't even waste time trying to convince them to cross. A dark wayward will play frustrating and confusing cat-and-mouse games, and can hide easily, because its vibrations are so much lower than those of a regular wayward. (For example, even though the man in *The Wayward and the Dragon* was gray, his depression made his vibrations so low that we didn't feel him for a long time.)

So, if we do encounter dark waywards, Colette and I just catch them in our psychic shields and hold them for the angels to take back home, where God deals with them. We learned this valuable lesson from Marie in *Our Pet Wayward*. (For a description of how to create a psychic shield, whether around your property or around your body, see page 164.) We have found that our personal shields can reach out about twenty feet in order to "grab" a dark one. The shield is part of our higher selves and can sense where a dark wayward is, but the ghost does have to be somewhat close (to us, or to our property) in order for the shield to grab it. I cannot stress enough the importance of keeping your personal shield up all the time, and making sure that it is strong. As long as you continue on your path and learn your lessons, your shield will continue to be healthy.

Once, however, Colette did try to convince a dark one to go to the light. He told her that he would go in a little while, if she would just let him go for the moment. Colette didn't fall for that trick, but kept him in her shield. (Dark ones can't hide their true nature forever; eventually, it comes out.) Colette eventually pushed him up. She knew that he wouldn't cross unless forced, but she wanted to see if she could make him see the error of his ways. He didn't, but now he's where he should be.

If you ever find yourself encountering a dark wayward that you are forced to deal with, our advice is to cross it quickly—grab it in your shield and keep it as far away from your physical body as possible. This is the only option, and the safest. This kind of crossing is rather traumatic for the wayward in question, but it is also the least traumatic for you (if you are going to become involved in crossing waywards, you really need to protect yourself and the other people around you first). Dark waywards are looking out only for themselves. If they see you as a threat to their freedom (and they will), they will try to get rid of you any way they can. Neither Colette nor I have ever tried to cross a dark way-ward by ourselves. We have always had each other or someone else around, to help us by lending their energy.

Once, Colette and I had a "stalker" dark one. He stayed just out of our reach and was able to avoid our attempts to capture him with our shields. We eventually called in help from the spirit world. From our studies in Wicca, we knew that there are lots of different dimensions and types of spirits; the spirits on the other side have much higher vibrations than dark waywards, so they're unable to help, but there are other spirits, like earth spirits, who have lower vibrations and therefore no trouble finding these dangerous ghosts. In this particular situation, Colette and I each called upon a particular type of earth spirit, and they were able to grab and hold the dark wayward (while we sent them extra energy for their effort) until we were able to grab it ourselves and cross it over.

This kind of forced crossing is justified, I believe, because the dark waywards have created trauma in other lives, both when they were physical and after going wayward. But in sharing our experience of dark waywards, I mostly want to convey a warning that there are these things out there, and you should try to avoid them. If you can't, protect yourself with your psychic shield.

Once you become involved in doing this kind of spiritual work, or any spiritual work for that matter, you can become a target for the dark side, in both a physical and a spiritual sense. Dark waywards will take advantage of any situation they can. They hold nothing sacred, and exist only to wreak havoc in our lives. They try to throw us off balance. When we are off balance and confused, we make mistakes and might get off our paths. This is their goal. They cannot turn a light soul dark, but they can cause us to experience depression and doubt about who we are and what we are doing, or need to do.

What's really scary is that dark waywards can be souls who have escaped from hell. These last ones are the most dangerous. They have a fresh memory of hell and they don't want to go back. Heaven can be almost as bad for them, because they would have to face the fact that they've gone off their path and need to make amends for what they've done and pay back karmic debt. Think about that for a while. Souls who have wreaked havoc in their own life, as well as in others' lives, will have to answer to themselves and God for where and when they went off their path.

Most dark waywards go directly to the left side, away from God and home. They stay there for a short time, then slingshot back into the physical world to the same life plan as when they went wrong. This is God's plan—Mom and Dad always give us another chance to get things right. But dark ones usually don't take advantage of this wonderful opportunity to make amends, and use their free-will choice to screw up again. Experienced ghost crossers try to catch these entities, once they're wayward, and send them back to God. This is definitely a case of "Let go and let God."

Conclusion

Waywards and "things that go bump in the night" used to frighten me, sometimes quite a bit. I suppose I was buying into the general Hollywood stereotype that ghosts are mean, vicious, and evil. This is not to say that we haven't met earth-bound souls who are like this; when someone becomes frustrated, confused, or hurt, he or she tends to strike out at anyone nearby. That was certainly what Mrs. Walton was doing, in the first story in this book. But when I learned that these poor individuals are just frightened because they don't understand what's happened to them, I realized that they just need a little compassion and a lot of love to help them go home. I taught this lesson to my daughter, and feel I can teach it to others as well.

Of course, I've had anxieties and misgivings about being able to do this kind of work, but I still had the desire and determination to do it anyway. So I began by taking small steps…and stumbling along, learning about the different souls (ghosts) that we met along the way. Yes, seeing the silhouette of a person at the end of your bed when you wake up in the middle of the night can be frightening, especially when the shadow disappears in front of your eyes. This kind of thing disturbs me still, for a short time. But then I realize that it's just someone asking for help, and I do what I can.

When I sat down to write this book, I knew where I would begin (with my first crossing, of course), but I had no idea how many waywards, of the hundreds we've crossed, to include (all the stories of our crossings are interesting to us, of course, since we lived them). So I began by picking out those stories that Colette and I learned the most from.

The first five stories in this book occurred early in my work. They demonstrate a wide variety of ways to cross earthbound souls. In *The Haunted House on Main Street* story, I realized that a ghost can manipulate the energy around it and be quite dangerous. I was even slightly injured when Mrs. Walton pushed me down the stairs. (I think that it gave her pause when my dog Nicky tried to help me up after I stopped my fall.) I still believe that Mrs. Walton tried other things, like driving my car into the fence and tree, but she didn't seem to try to hurt me again. The lightbulbs that blew out and exploded in my bedroom were intended more to frighten than harm me.

With Nimbi, in the *Commitments* story, I learned more about desire and determination when it came to dealing with an earthbound soul. While Mrs. Walton was angry that people were living in "her" house without invitation, Nimbi was just plain scared. He needed a gentle but firm hand to get him to the light. Communication from the other side had come in the form of a dream that helped me to know what to do, and what not to do, in order to cross him.

Marie, in *Our Pet Wayward*, was even more frightened than Nimbi. She ultimately warmed up to us, and we were able to help her after that. Marie was with us for the longest time of any of the earthbound souls we dealt with, but we needed to learn a lot at that time and she, however unwittingly, obliged. Probably the most important thing Marie taught us was how to program our shields to protect ourselves against the dark ones. Feeling afraid can give you an edge if you use it to your advantage, but uncontrolled fear can paralyze you and cause harm—great harm sometimes. Realizing this during our work with Marie helped us learn about the dark waywards we would eventually be coming into contact with.

The Walmart Waywards taught Colette and me to think on our feet, and to do further research in order to help better. Most of these earthbound souls had been young and/or mentally impaired in the physical world, so the idea of a party with cake and ice cream sounded good to them, especially since there were no nurses or doctors at the party.

When I met *The Men in Gray*, we were able not only to close the psychic portal that fools had opened in the graveyard, but we'd learned enough about dark waywards to grab one in our shield and push him up. But it was in dealing with the confederate soldier waywards that I really began to realize how important pop culture is in communicating with the other side. By reading books, listening to music, and watching television and movies, you can get insights from the spirit world, and thus solve problems that come up in daily life. This principle applies to all sorts of things, I've found, not just helping waywards home.

Conclusion

The collection of stories in *Quick Waywards*, of course, are example of times when Colette and I were reminded that we don't always have to work long or hard or think deeply about crossing some earthbound souls. Sometimes it's just as simple as saying "Go to the light." This is always the first thing we try when we become aware of a ghost around us. It's also the easiest way to help a wayward (we are all about "easy" when the situation presents itself!).

In *Candi's Mother-in-Law*, I learned that my religious beliefs can be beneficial when it comes to helping a wayward to the light. We usually try to avoid using our Wiccan beliefs or the religion itself to cross an earthbound soul, but sometimes it can be helpful.

The next stories are some of the ones I consider the most interesting—*Our Favorite Ghost Stories*, or the funny stories. I hope these tales give you a wide variety of ideas about ways to cross waywards, as well as show you that, while Colette and I take this work seriously, it's not always serious work. Some of the *Quick Waywards* stories are also an example of this—I still can't believe I challenged a ghost to shit on my head if he didn't like the other side! But as long as it works and you don't lie to the wayward, that's all that matters.

The last five stories all occurred while I was in the process of writing this book. *Elizabeth* came to us just before I got the idea about sharing my experiences this way, and was very helpful in restoring my faith in what my daughter and I do with waywards. I had some expectations about Elizabeth, at first; I more or less expected her to "behave" herself, but she tried to distract me in front of customers at my job. After getting to know her, however, I realized that this was just part of Elizabeth's personality, which made me appreciate her that much more. In no way do Colette and I ever try to break a ghost's "spirit," so to speak. We just try to make the soul realize that what he or she really want is on the other side of the light.

Conclusion

My experience with *Pool Hall Jenny* really drove home to me that ghosts are people too. She was more "alive" after her death than some of the physical people I've met. Ever since meeting Jenny, I've tried to emulate her, living in the moment and enjoying life as much as I can. The earthbound soul in *The Wayward and the Dragon*, meanwhile, frightened both my daughter and me, but we bucked it up and took him on. His guilt and fear were making him angry at intruders, but the kindly dragon helped to alleviate these emotions through love. Lastly, I wasn't too worried about the old woman attached to our washing machine in *Music Soothes the Earthbound Soul* (she was harmless enough, just lonely), but the big African American wayward I noticed at Mark and Anna's house did concern me due to all the electricity that was pulsing around us at the P.O.D. concert, especially since it was humid. Fortunately, I had help from God in the form of angels. It was still the wayward's choice to leave the physical plane and go home, but I felt that the angels were there to safeguard the physical people at the concert.

Crossing waywards to the other side continues to be a work in progress. It is also a labor of love (and occasionally a labor of frustration, with the stubborn waywards). I hope that you, my reader, have enjoyed this book and can use it as a type of learning tool, or guide, in crossing earthbound souls to the other side. Colette and I did a lot of inner path-walking, meditation, and learning by trial and error (as demonstrated in *Our Pet Wayward*) in the process of learning to do this incredible volunteer job. Prayer has been a huge part of our success. Talking to God is a good thing!

I'm not saying that you won't encounter challenges in this work, and we definitely encourage everyone to do this job for his or her own benefit, but we hope our book has taken some of the guesswork out of helping ghosts … of helping those among us who need a little understanding and direction.

Conclusion

As far as I know, this is the only book that can be used as a teaching tool for this odd occupation. One cannot be graded on crossing ghosts—success is based mainly on desire and determination. Good intentions, based in love, are the prerequisites for this job.

One last caution ... before you cross a wayward on private property, please get permission from the owner to be there. As in the *Commitments* story, I had permission from my friend Jane to come to her house. I did not, however, have permission from my daughter's friends, or their mother, to come onto the property where Marcella was, so I stayed on the sidewalk. Although I didn't tell Mark and Anna at first that I was crossing dark waywards, they had invited me to their house and I had permission to be there (sometimes the information about the spiritual work is best kept to oneself). Again, please do not trespass. Most of the ghosts we found were either on public property or were drawn to us. Either way, do not break any laws while trying to cross earthbound souls to the other side. It kind of defeats the idea of loving your neighbor!

Suggested Reading

Dreams

Browne, Sylvia, with Lindsay Harrison. *Sylvia Browne's Book of Dreams*. New York: Dutton, 2002.

Summer Rain, Mary, with Alex Greystone. *Mary Summer Rain on Dreams: A Quick-Reference Guide to over 14,500 Dream Symbols*. Norfolk, VA: Hampton Roads Publishing Co., 1996.

Ghosts

Summer Rain, Mary. *Phantoms Afoot: Helping the Spirits Among Us*. Norfolk, VA: Hampton Roads Publishing Co., 1993.

Van Praagh, James. *Ghosts Among Us: Uncovering the Truth About the Other Side*. New York: Harper Collins, 2008.

Guided Meditation

Browne, Sylvia. *Soul's Perfection*. Carlsbad, CA: Hay House, 2002.

———, with Lindsay Harrison. *The Other Side and Back: A Psychic's Guide to Our World and Beyond*. New York: Dutton, 1999.

Puryear, Herbert B. *The Edgar Cayce Primer: Discovering the Path to Self-Transformation*. New York: Bantam, 1982.

Reincarnation/Past Lives

Browne, Sylvia, with Lindsay Harrison. *Past Lives, Future Healing: A Psychic Reveals the Secrets to Good Health and Great Relationships*. New York: Dutton, 2001.

Langley, Noel, under the editorship of Hugh Lynn Cayce. *Edgar Cayce on Reincarnation*. New York: Warner Books, 1967.

Spirits

Konstantinos. *Speak with the Dead: Seven Methods for Spirit Communication*. St. Paul, MN: Llewellyn Publications, 2005.

Wicca (the basics)

Cunningham, Scott. *The Truth About Witchcraft Today*. St. Paul, MN: Llewellyn Publications, 1988.

RavenWolf, Silver. *Teen Witch: Wicca for a New Generation*. St. Paul, MN: Llewellyn Publications, 1988.

Wicca (more advanced)

McCoy, Edain. *Advanced Witchcraft: Go Deeper, Reach Further, Fly Higher*. St. Paul, MN: Llewellyn Publications, 2004.

Wood, Gail. *Sisters of the Dark Moon: 13 Rituals of the Dark Goddess*. St. Paul, MN: Llewellyn Publications, 2001.

To Write to the Author

If you wish to contact the author or would like more information about this book, please write to the author in care of Llewellyn Worldwide and we will forward your request. Both the author and publisher appreciate hearing from you and learning of your enjoyment of this book and how it has helped you. Llewellyn Worldwide cannot guarantee that every letter written to the author can be answered, but all will be forwarded. Please write to:

Anson V. Gogh
℅ Llewellyn Worldwide
2143 Wooddale Drive, Dept. 978-0-7387-1935-1
Woodbury, MN 55125-2989, U.S.A.

Please enclose a self-addressed stamped envelope for reply,
or $1.00 to cover costs. If outside the U.S.A., enclose an
international postal reply coupon.

Many of Llewellyn's authors have websites with additional information and resources. For more information, please visit our website at http://www.llewellyn.com.